In Defence of Barbarism

The journalist Louisa Yousfi grew up in south-eastern France in the 1990s. She took a literature course at a crammer in Lille and then studied philosophy in Nice, ultimately enrolling in journalism school in Bordeaux. She was a conscientious student, following the advice of her working-class parents, who had emigrated from Algeria to France, to 'focus on [her] studies first and worry about politics later'. This political engagement duly materialized when she joined the Parti des Indigènes de la République, an anti-racist and decolonial movement whose ideas had a decisive influence on her first published work, *Rester barbare*. She is currently working on her first novel.

In Defence of Barbarism

Non-Whites against the Empire

Louisa Yousfi

Translated by Andy Bliss

VERSO

London • New York

This book is supported by the Institut français
(Royaume-Uni) as part of the Burgess programme.

This English-language edition published by Verso 2025
Originally published in French as *Rester barbare*
by La fabrique éditions 2022
© Louisa Yousfi 2022
Translation © Andy Bliss 2025

1 3 5 7 9 10 8 6 4 2

Verso
UK: 6 Meard Street, London W1F 0EG
US: 207 East 32nd Street, New York, NY 10016
versobooks.com

Verso is the imprint of New Left Books

ISBN-13: 978-1-80429-442-0
ISBN-13: 978-1-80429-444-4 (US EBK)
ISBN-13: 978-1-80429-443-7 (UK EBK)

British Library Cataloguing in Publication Data
A catalogue record for this book is available from the British Library

Library of Congress Cataloging-in-Publication Data

Names: Yousfi, Louisa, 1989- author. | Bliss, Andy, translator.
Title: In defence of barbarism : non-whites against the Empire / Louisa
 Yousfi ; translated by Andy Bliss.
Other titles: Rester barbare. English | Non-whites against the Empire
Description: English-language edition. | London ; New York : Verso, 2024. |
 "Originally published in French as Rester barbare by La fabrique
 éditions 2022." | Includes bibliographical references and index.
Identifiers: LCCN 2024034385 (print) | LCCN 2024034386 (ebook) | ISBN
 9781804294420 (paperback) | ISBN 9781804294444 (US ebk)
Subjects: LCSH: Black people--France--Attitudes. | France--Race relations.
Classification: LCC DC34.5.B55 Y6813 2024 (print) | LCC DC34.5.B55
 (ebook) | DDC 305.896/073044--dc23/eng/20241004
LC record available at https://lccn.loc.gov/2024034385
LC ebook record available at https://lccn.loc.gov/2024034386

Typeset in Sabon by MJ & N Gavan, Truro, Cornwall
Printed and bound by CPI Group (UK) Ltd, Croydon, CR0 4YY

By living in the shadows, we have ended up entering into a pact with the monsters and grubs that lurk there. It's time to break this pact and look boldly into the light – stare this Barbary sun in the face.

Mohammed Dib, *God in Barbary*

To Mum, who would scold me for
writing these wicked words.

To Dad, who would smile.

Contents

Acknowledgements

To Houria Bouteldja, whom I hold in the highest esteem. Thank you for being the first to take the leap.

To Anthony F., who taught me how to break some rules. Thank you for *the real life*.

To Kateb and Mansour, for their voracious engagement.

To my disruptive influences: La Pince, Godot, Gavroche, Le Dandy, and Rockfeller.

To my publishers, and, in particular, Stella Magliani-Belkacem for her trust, wisdom, and sterling friendship.

To Félix Boggio Éwanjé-Épée, for his sorcerer's gifts.

To the PIR campaigners, thanks to whom I have unlearned everything.

1

A Certain Barbarism

I bear witness to a people that is no longer hailed in keeping with its true force and stature.
– Sony Labou Tansi, *Encre, sueur, salive et sang*[1]

By his own admission, Kateb Yacine is a barbarian. With disarming directness, he declared in an interview: 'I feel I've got so many things to say that I'm better off not being too cultivated. I have to retain a certain barbarism, I need to remain a barbarian.'[2] It's a beautiful and striking phrase that you immediately feel you understand. Culture is a form of gluttony that makes the mind obese and impotent. Barbarianism is a primitive vitality that produces authentic writing, pure creative acts, and poetry. It's perversely tempting to give it an erudite spin by suggesting that Kateb Yacine is resurrecting Nietzsche's Apollonian–Dionysian duality in order to express the inner tensions of the creative act – between order and chaos, restraint and hubris: in short, between culture and barbarism. But such musings belong to the world of comfortable armchairs and earnest chin-stroking that is the very antithesis of the 'certain barbarianism' that you have to hang on to if you have 'things to say'. No, we don't want to go down that road with his magic formula.

Who is Kateb Yacine when he says he has to 'remain'

a barbarian and 'retain' a certain barbarism? That is the crucial question. Kateb Yacine was an Algerian who was reduced to the status of 'native' (*indigène*) under the French colonial administration. But he came from a family of dignitaries and thus enjoyed the peculiar status of belonging to the indigenous elite, meaning that he could attend a French school and learn the history, literature, poetry, and language of the colonial empire. Transposing him to the present day, we would say that he was an *integrated* native: a pure product of a French state education, he had an effortless mastery of the language, could quote Victor Hugo verbatim and exchange pleasantries with the French. But he had so many 'things to say' that he sensed that a cultured conversation was not fertile ground for honing his art. Having things to say has nothing to do with conversing pleasantly. The barbarian always *breaks into* a conversation. Stealing the floor from the well-spoken, he injects fresh vigour into the conversation by transfiguring it into an event – or, more precisely, into an assault. That is the essence of the Katebian aesthetic: barbarism as the locus of self-expression from which the jarring poet-boxer wrecks the established order to reveal the naked truth about it. But, however accurate that may be, we risk falling back into academic mode. And, in any case, that's not all there is to the Kateb Yacine formula, and we need to wheedle the full meaning out of it. To reveal not only what it expresses for the author himself and his enlightened conscience but also what it 'has to say' to those of us who experience a shiver of confused complicity when we encounter it. What does this phrase tell us about ourselves – about me personally? For it has an impact on us not merely as an aesthetic prescription – 'I need to remain a barbarian' – but as a political narrative.

For a start, there are the verbs he uses: to retain and remain. They're interesting in that they denote a prior time. They suggest Kateb Yacine was originally a barbarian before becoming a respected man of letters. In fact, they go further and suggest that he is in the process of losing that original barbarism – a dramatic development for both the man and the poet who has 'things to say'. But what exactly is the barbarian losing when caught up in the march of progress of a civilization that has endowed them with the cultural riches that are the pride of empires, not least the superb French language steeped in centuries of history? That person has probably found in this language a means of expressing their genius and been warmly applauded for it by the French themselves. What exactly is being lost by Kateb Yacine, the Algerian native whom the Parisian literati champion as the 'Algerian Rimbaud'? Lovers of the French poet will perhaps exclaim, 'Harar!'[3] The analogy might be irresistible, but Yacine has his own distinct experience of barbarism – literally, not metaphorically.

He may have been a member of the native aristocracy, but he took to the streets of Sétif in protest at French colonialism on 8 May 1945. He was sixteen years old and joined the nationalist demonstrations organized to coincide with the festivities celebrating the Allied victory. What happened next is well documented: a terrible carnage in which several tens of thousands of Algerians lost their lives on the day itself and during the brutal crackdown that followed. Yacine escaped death but not prison, and he identifies his detention as the point at which he first came into contact with the 'true' Algeria in flesh and blood: a battered and dehumanized people whose will to revolt was nevertheless unshakeable. Above all, this was the foundational moment in his decision to become a public writer, a scribe, a *kateb*.[4] He resolved to write among the illiterate for the illiterate, or 'in place of the illiterate' as Deleuze would say, in order to avenge his race of barbarians.

In the eyes of the colonial administration, that was exactly what they were: an inferior species stuck at a primitive stage of human development, a formless and morally abject mass. When they seem inoffensive, they are primitive folk. When they revolt, they are barbarians. This is not an anodyne distinction, and we shall be returning to it. What we need to note for now is that 'barbarian' is a historical identity pinned on him at birth that becomes like a second skin. But it is not (yet) a shell – far from it. It is a kind of banishment imposed by Western civilization. Beyond the Empire, it is the zone of non-being where he vegetates with his fellow detainees, among them farmers, students, and revolutionary comrades. Barbarians all. His social status does nothing to alter that. It is in prison that he realizes that he has never left this zone, that all his efforts to speak the language of the civilizer and master the codes of their world count for nothing in the face of this basic truth: a barbarian I am, and a barbarian I shall remain. This revelation prompts him to make a vow: a barbarian I am, and a barbarian I *wish* to remain. He opens a breach in the insult levelled at him, and indeed he turns out to be adept at this: seizing the enemy's weapon and turning it against them. The French language becomes one of the spoils of war. The codes of the French novel are shattered into a 'starred polygon'.[5] Barbarism is a source of pride. This strategy for parrying insults is as old as oppression itself: you catch them in mid-air, subvert them, and flip their meaning entirely. It might sound simple, but such an approach has its perils and requires a certain art. There are, however, many alchemist peoples who have performed this miracle of transforming stigma into a source of pride, infamy into something noble. If you needed to sum it up in a slogan, it would be: 'Yes, so …?' This is another magic formula: 'Barbarian, yes, so …?' Contrary to appearances, that 'yes' does not endorse anything. It's having fun, it's amusing itself like an insolent kid who's mastered the art of antagonizing. When they've stopped laughing, they look their accuser directly in the eye and conclude with a disorientating *yes, so …?* that says: another game is in progress here, a secret game whose rules you don't know. Can't you just feel the breath of fresh air? You'd think a huge window has just been opened in the middle of winter. The air may be glacial, a real slap in the face. But, my word, it enables us to breathe. You could create a dictionary of these phrases, which you might call *The Dictionary of Magic Formulas*, subtitle: *The Negro Tells You to Go to Hell*. Well, the barbarian is telling you to go to hell too, and what a breath of fresh air that is.

The truth is, we're suffocating. Here's what happens. There's a long history of domesticating barbarians. In the language of the Empire, this is called integration. At the end of it all, we no longer say, 'yes, so …?' but rather, 'it's not even true'. The defence of a kid who lacks cunning. To prove our human credentials, we think we have to reassure those who doubt them. Look at us, we're just like you! We're forever bending over backwards to adopt as our own their codes, manners, and culture, which we force-feed ourselves in one binge after another. But however much we do this, we're always lagging behind. In the end, it spills out everywhere because it hasn't been digested properly. And you have to admit that there's something odd about someone with barbarian features trying to speak posh. If only the stain could be removed, but the performance is all in vain and, if you look closely, it's even rather pathetic. All these personal contortions and automaton grimaces just to say: *we are human beings like them*. Though we take care not to ask the question that trumps all others: who do we mean by *them* anyway? Stamp Paid, the black character in *Beloved* who helps runaway slaves, doesn't beat about the bush, asking bluntly: 'What *are* these people?'[6] It's a good question. Do those doing the dehumanizing even have the humanity which they believe gives them the right to assess the souls of others? Do they even have souls themselves? It's striking how suddenly this becomes a scandalous question. It's like imagining the bodies of white children washed up on Mediterranean beaches – another reversal of perspective that lays the world bare. The rules of the game are defective, because the more we try to prove our humanity, the more the suspicion grows. The very act of justifying ourselves implies that the doubts were well grounded in the first place and always will be. 'Yes, so ...?' is the only worthy response. Shatter everything and sabotage the visible border as well as the invisible one that separates *within* the Empire itself the legitimate children from us dirty boys and girls who have been desperately spewed out into this world. Simply crossing a border is not enough to eradicate it – who could still believe in such a myth? This is something the first-, second-, and umpteenth-generation gang (whether we're naturalized or citizens by birth right, with our two passports and yet at risk of being stripped of our nationality) know only too well: to cross their border without destroying it is to perpetuate it and block the path of other randomly designated barbarians behind us. This is the story of the *beur* (second- or third-generation North Africans living in France) and the *blédard* (people from a North African background), the *harraga* (illegal North African migrants to Europe), the native, and the damned of the Earth.[7] The rupture with what went before is structured and fervently encouraged. Even the most ardent defenders of the Empire are prepared to negotiate: alright, we'll let you in, but not them. Deal? That's how betrayal comes about – it's simply how the world works. The potential for betrayal is inherent in a border; we might try to distance ourselves from this cruelty, but it will eventually catch up with us, along with the image of those bodies washed up on the beach. We catch ourselves saying 'our' beaches, and then it's already too late. We'll soon be saying at *our* gates, at *our* borders. That's what's called successful integration: when their barbarians become ours too. The marine cemetery haunts us because it is the truth of our condition. How do we hang on to the South? Our unease is increased by the complex that we have about our privileged status, even as we ask ourselves: how do we save what remains of us?

In his own way, Kateb Yacine was haunted too. His obsession with the illiterate and the grassroots of his country was ultimately a reflection of that. He felt that he could lose Algeria and betray it, and, indeed, that he was being encouraged to do so – not only by flesh-and-blood human beings and the Establishment, but by a certain moral order structuring the world. The civilized and the barbarians. Humanity and its monstrous margins. He felt all that, and so he made a choice: to retain a certain barbarism. To retain and to remain – verbs of preservation and resistance. For Kateb Yacine resists. He resists his acculturation as well as his disintegration. Even as he distances himself from

7

his people – an inevitable consequence of being a writer and hence part of the 'World Republic of Letters', he is anxious not to lose his way.[8] Here's another phrase for the dictionary: 'I know where I'm from'. This is the phrase of a defector that expresses a border crossed and the process of going up in the world. And, above all, it means that once I'm up there, I won't forget my lowly origins. It's an oath of loyalty to those we've left behind. But it takes on an extra magic in the context of barbarism, because in truth we don't know where these barbarians – where we – come from. What exactly is this original barbarism that we're supposed to be retaining? That question has us groping for an answer because we don't know. How do we mourn an authenticity that we have never known and yet genuinely lost? What is this urge to preserve something that we can't put our finger on? People nudge us and whisper: it's identity politics and we shouldn't give in to it. It's an evanescent and paradoxical feeling: a nostalgia for something that never took place. Doesn't everyone from an immigrant background feel this, deep down? Feel that something is slowly leaving them forever as they become more integrated? It's an impossible feeling that raises a vast array of questions, all of which start with the words *what would we have become if only …?* If only colonization hadn't established a moral order that holds in check the civilization, country, and family within which we should have been born and grown up? If only the integrationist perspective hadn't dictated the conditions for our salvation in this country with conditions attached that feels nothing like a homeland? What would we have become if only …?

In the political arena, such questions would seem absurd; they would be sacrificed on the altar of historical materialism and condemned for encouraging people to idolize a fantasy golden age, to erect into a dogma a fabricated precolonial authenticity. Communism has its infantile disease, and so the decolonization movement must have one too. 'What next? What are you going to do with this identity once you have patched it back together?', we are asked. 'Use it against us? Impose it on us?' It's at once sad and fascinating to observe the obsessive scrutiny of any sign that might remotely hint at a desire for vengeance. We're used to the panicked reactions, and the attempts to discredit movements that seek to translate the *yes, so …?* into a political strategy. There's similar panic when it is claimed that these decolonializing types, these self-proclaimed barbarians, are trying to recast race relations, but this time in their favour. They fail to understand that our question – 'What would we have become if only …?' – does not call for an answer. In truth, it's less a question of rediscovering what we *were* than resisting what we are in the process of *becoming*. From this perspective, the 'certain barbarism' that we wish to hold on to is precisely that which has not been affected – contaminated – by our integration into the Empire. It's the wasteland in us, our virgin land. This is also why it's not about becoming a barbarian, but remaining one and accepting the political truth contained in the term: deep down, what they are afraid of is not that we might lack humanity, culture, or a moral sense, but the precise opposite. They are afraid of that part of us that cannot be assimilated, which is to say our history, our culture, and our soul. For what kind of a barbarian is it, they ask, who would reflect on their innermost character, their values, and their beauty? Who is this contemplative barbarian who wants to build museums and formulate a new ethical perspective?

At this point, we need to pause for a moment because words are viscous and can slip through our fingers. A barbarian is not a savage. Whereas the barbarian is beyond saving, the savage can be civilized. Their innocence has nothing to do with the barbarian's wasteland; it is a childlike innocence that arises from their primitive human status. For this reason, savages cannot be held entirely responsible when they err. Some civilizing types will even whip their own backs, so to speak, to alleviate the savage's responsibility. This is a master's attitude: it's their duty to educate the good savages – the eternal victims – and elevate them to human status. It's the line taken by our many unwelcome advocates and false allies.

'I'm not a man to be civilized, but to take or leave just as I am' is the response of Sony Labou Tansi.[9] These are the words of a barbarian who in no sense exists prior to civilization or in the absence thereof. Barbarians are products of this civilization but not reducible to it. Their existence testifies to an unplanned mutation that is not encoded in the civilizing process. One might even say that they are *ahead* of civilization. They are figures of the future, from the future. You could do amazing things with that concept: grandiose tales of rebel peoples travelling back from the future to save the world from itself; of splendid barbarians from hooded tribes demanding independence; of Siamese twins working as night watchmen at the top of the Eiffel Tower; of black pirates lording it over the waves just as Resistance fighters ruled the *maquis* – tales that really lift the spirits. That can be done, and is done, but not by the more domesticated barbarians. Look at how eager they are instead to defuse their oddness by reaching for the well-worn motif of being caught between two stools.

God knows why we thought this could be a source of pride for us. *We are enriched by two cultures. We are a hyphen between the two shores of the Mediterranean, between East and West.*[10] Blah, blah, blah. Who wants to be a damn hyphen? Abdelkebir Khatibi complained about this: 'Poor Arab, where did you end up, reduced to a series of hyphens!'[11] A hyphen does not enhance our value; it's merely putting a brave face on our predicament. Franco-something doesn't mean we're doubly privileged, it means we're going extinct because this hyphen links nothing. It sets out instead the terms of an unequal war between the bombers and the cradles.[12] Who do you suppose is going to win? The Franco- or the -something? The clue is in the question. Gradual integration into the Empire is what this hyphen denotes – a line on the page to which the second part clings, but for how much longer? But we cling to it not because we believe in the fable it represents, but because we know which of the two parts either side of the hyphen will be sacrificed if our conditions of existence force us to choose. And this, in turn, tells us which part we really hold dear: that part where our historical substance and our grassroots lie.

This book is dedicated to the contemporary barbarians whose lives and works teach us more than any academic treatise can about what the Empire calls the 'regression into savagery'.[13] And on the front line we find the street prophets, since all these contemporary tales – the black pirate and the Siamese-twin night watchmen – come to us from the margins of the Empire and its recalcitrant members.[14] Both unbowed and well versed in the laws of the Empire, the genius of rappers lies in their ability to create a new mythology of the barbarian condition, appropriating the tropes of European horror for their own ends. Even the ostensibly inoffensive fable of being caught between two stools assumes a destructive dimension when it comes into contact with their world. They also say, 'We are straddling two worlds, one that is dying and another that is taking its time to integrate us completely' – but they don't need Gramsci to tell them that 'monsters will emerge from this chiaroscuro'. These monsters have to be dissected so that we can ascertain their genealogy, understand how they work, and sift the fiction from the reality, beauty from ugliness, and the act of resistance from death. It is something of a minefield that demands a new language specifically designed for the task. Hence Kateb Yacine and his magic formula. Hence Aimé Césaire. Hence Toni Morrison, Abdelkebir Khatibi, and Sony Labou Tansi. Hence the need to give ourselves the time to understand, to place our faith in the storyteller, and to allow ourselves to be swept up in a beautiful story. Once upon a time there were the civilized ones, the monsters, and the barbarians. Title: *Ya, Franssa* (Oh, France).[15] Subtitle: *What have you turned us into?*

2

Black Man Kills White Woman

'Your trouble, son', his thoughts continued without interruption. 'You tried too hard to please. Showed right there you were a primitive. A human being never tries to please. Not restricted by conscience like a primitive. Reason why he's human.'

– Chester Himes, *The End of a Primitive*[1]

Jesse Robinson has just killed Kriss Cummings. Before calling the police to give himself up, he shaves and spends some time tying a perfect knot in his tie. Examining himself in the mirror, he now feels ready to confront them: 'I'm a nigger, and I've just killed a white woman.'[2]

This is how Chester Himes's novel *The End of a Primitive* concludes, with a perfect sentence: black man kills white woman. It has the perfection of a truism because when he writes that, what we automatically read is: guilty man kills innocent woman. It's a narrative tautology. 'What do you mean?', Chester Himes seems to be saying with a snigger. A guilty man who finally behaves like a guilty man, isn't that what you wanted? 'End product of the impact of Americanization on one Jesse Robinson – black man. Your answer son. You've been searching for it. BLACK MAN KILLS WHITE WOMAN. All the proof you need now.'[3]

Chester Himes is not a novelist; he's a torturer. The

kind who smashes his reader's head open to reveal all the filth inside. All the dark nooks and crannies, shameful thoughts, and sophisticated contortions to hide them. He plunges his big hands inside, and we look on in horror as he unwraps his haul like a packet of tripe: this is what you are, this is what we are. We're all screwed, we're falling apart. But the system is in fine shape. He implicitly presents this macabre dénouement as a triumph, though not one of racial vengeance, as we might be inclined to think. This is the triumph of the prevailing moral order – of an unrelenting and implacably rational system whose tragic workings he depicts with surgical precision. 'You knew it two days before it happened. Perhaps two years. Perhaps from the time they first hurt you for being born black.'[4]

Jesse Robinson might not be born 'primitive', but this insult gradually makes its influence felt in every fibre of his being. Worse still, he feels powerless to constrain the monster that is forever swelling inside him. It is pulsating like blood beneath the skin, and he is going to end up acting like a primitive for real. And so, as if to conjure it up, he manically anticipates the crime he is about to commit: 'Bitch wants to die.'[5] The narrative tension captures a deadly eroticism running out of control, with all his energies converging towards a single explosion and point of release: the white woman has to be killed. Even Kriss herself, turned on by the idea of being treated like a racial archetype, seems to be yearning for her own death – a white woman rehabilitated in death, which is to say, killed by the black man she has demeaned herself by sleeping with. 'Now we're all even, baby', declares Jesse beside her inert body.[6] And, in this infernal confrontation between two antithetical archetypes of the modern racial order – the black man and the white woman – everything is indeed in order. The primitive has acted like a primitive. The white woman has died like a white woman. Jesse Robinson hands himself in to the police without flinching and will take his place in prison alongside the thousands of other black men who have been rotting there since the dawn of time. And history can get ready to play itself out all over again.

Such is the moral matrix of Chester Himes's oeuvre: the racist worldview is an endlessly self-fulfilling loop that creates the conditions for its perpetual repetition. The black man is going to kill the white woman, and so he must be persecuted, discriminated against, and humiliated, in order to suppress his urge to avenge … his persecution, discrimination, and humiliation. Racism wrecks its victims so that they behave exactly as predicted by the grand narrative of the Empire: as a brutal, vengeful Other, as a primitive. But Chester Himes's fiction doesn't simply *address* the question – it tunnels into the contradictions and ultimately *becomes* the contradiction, exposing a blinding truth. In staging a racial murder as the inevitable logical culmination of what has come before, Himes appropriates the codes of literary tragedy and applies them to the race issue. It's no longer 'Venus entire' but 'racial hatred entire' that is 'latched onto its prey'.[7] Jean Racine deploys this metaphor to convey the idea that Phèdre is responsible for, but not guilty of, her sin, and Himes accords his hero the same treatment while introducing an original twist: the fate of Jesse Robinson is not inscribed in the heavens, but rather is an immanent destiny. Racism is the modern incarnation of fate, and its victims are the tragic heroes of our age.

So, when people try to sum up what they suppose the message of Chester Himes's oeuvre to be, they will say:

racism – by perverting the soul of its victims, nurturing within them a furious monster, *prompting their regression into savagery* – results in the enactment of the very threat it is supposed to prevent, thereby perpetuating itself.

And that's true as far as it goes. But, the more you think about it, the more you realize that this really doesn't do justice to Himes's incendiary lucidity. To appreciate this fully, we need only observe how reassuring such a reading is, to everyone – and how it serves to defuse tensions. It may be an original and even bold interpretation, but it doesn't effect a rupture, and may even build bridges, at the other end of which, and not so far away sadly, we can make out a whole gaggle of sociologists earnestly acquiescing – all those people who are working on the *question*, as they delicately put it (rather than saying outright: our ugly side). How come we are so immoral, violent, and downright mad inside our skulls? That's their real bloody question. And if they nevertheless dare to ask it, it's because they feel their answer will exonerate them from any charge of malice towards us. Besides, that answer is there for all to see, confirmed and endorsed by that great expert in the defects of his own race, Mr Chester Himes himself. Our villainy, our moral turpitude and our purported tendency to concentrate all the vices of humanity, to give into our atavistic bellicose instincts, to beat the women and children we love, to hang around the streets looking for criminal opportunities, to fire into crowds, and to lynch gays and spit on Jews – all of this is apparently down to something lacking in our lives. All those things we supposedly never had, all the opportunities that were never available, all that recognition we were deprived of, all the love we never received. And the compassion they ooze when they think they are giving us back our dignity, the emotion they tremble with in recounting our sorry tale! Their conclusion is that we've remained stuck at the age when love was absent for us. What they're really trying to understand is why we're so ugly and they're so beautiful, but of course this is not how they picture it to themselves. They have a way of putting things that avoids any self-scrutiny. But we who live in the nether world with its nether language know how to translate what they're saying.

So, spare us your tears. Barbarians are not savages who should have been whipped and humiliated less, and cuddled more – savages that civilization left behind. Observe how proud they are of their critical faculties when they assert that we are *only* the sum of our frustrations, *only* the product of what their world has refused to give us. But they're not as smart as they think when they claim to defend us by citing our vulnerability, madness, irresponsibility, and bestiality. After all (they implicitly seem to be saying), man and beast are not judged by the same standards, are they? They may see themselves as clever advocates for our cause, but, in fact, they act like judges who condemn us to remain victims – their victims, devoid of moral sophistication and psychological depth. This is their major discovery: they believe that our 'regression into savagery' is down to the failure of integration. To save us from our monsters, they need to integrate us better. They need to allow us finally to sit at their table, albeit while treating us with kid gloves, as though we were children, sick people, or refugees, with our broken little lives. And woe betide the barbarian who turns down the invitation! The real enemies, they warn us, are those who defend the opposite point of view: that we are ontologically guilty, that *guilt is something we suckle along with milk at our mother's breast*. In whichever direction we look, the net seems to be tightening around us and threatening to disfigure us. 'Wimps or monsters': there's no more accurate phrase to describe the tragic condition of the barbarian.[8]

Backed into a corner by the deliberate provocations of his mistress, who takes her frustrations out on him, and the rejection by his publisher and society more generally, Jesse Robinson makes his choice. Live like a wimp? He'd rather croak. As it snaps shut on him, the existential trap he is in reveals the full extent of its cruelty: the path of resistance is exactly the same as the one that leads to his inner ruin. He is trapped in an impossible dichotomy: defending his honour means becoming a monster. It is an unending, unrelenting, totalitarian nightmare: 'Not only natural, plausible, logical, inevitable, psychiatrically compulsive and sociologically conclusive behaviour of a human being – and all the rest of the shit the social scientists think up – but mathematically accurate and politically correct as well.'[9]

We really are as screwed as can be. When we think we're rebelling, we're in fact destroying ourselves. When we look to assert ourselves, we're repudiating ourselves. Jesse laughs and Jesse cries in front of his mirror in a jumble of emancipation and horror, beauty and ugliness. And just you try untangling all that – it's impossible. The knot is as tight as a clenched fist, and sometimes we try hitting the wall with it. And what does that make us look like? A bunch of lunatics, or at best suspicious individuals who need to be watched very closely. Aren't we bound to end up believing in our own ugliness and giving into it, telling ourselves that it's the result of social determinism? And what are we supposed to do when we get to that stage? The tragedy is that we *already* believe it deep down inside. When we speak of ourselves between ourselves, we implicitly admit it to each other. Never in front of witnesses, of course. But, between ourselves, we speak of it as if to say: we know what we're like. When all hell is breaking loose outside, we whisper to ourselves that inevitable conclusion: an Arab again, no doubt. And we feel a bit ashamed. It's true that it's sometimes a relief to fall back on the sociological narrative and list all the misfortunes associated with being poorly integrated, all the injustices we have suffered, all the contempt and the rejection. And we believe it, not least because, in a sense, it's true. But, deep down, we still privately think there's something not quite right about us, *specifically* about us. *We're not normal.* And those poor civilized types have to put up with us. That's how my mum talks. She's ashamed on account of all the stupid things Arabs do in this country. *The poor things*, she says of 'real' French people, *the poor things have to put up with us.* She believes that, one day, they'll stop putting up with us and we'll pay for having been so ugly while they were so beautiful. They might then become a little ugly themselves, but it will only be to bring us into line and then they can become beautiful again, as if nothing has happened. She's already experienced that as a native in Algeria. They now pretend that nothing happened, but she can remember what they're really like beneath their good manners. We all know it on some level, but we tend to gloss over it and find them splendid most of the time. The veneer of civilization maintains the illusion. How are you supposed to compete with Western civilization, anyway? It invented innocence; it massacres entire peoples and creates Walt Disney while it's about it. Up against all that, how are we, the pathetic ugly ones, supposed to carry on respecting and liking ourselves?

How do we avoid victim-mentality resentment; indeed, how do we avoid losing it all together and going on the rampage?

Quit blubbing, says Jesse to himself in front of the mirror, adding: 'It's funny really. You just got to get the handle to the joke.'[10] And Jesse does indeed have an answer to it all, a hell of an answer. The trick is to complete the truncated title *The End of a Primitive*. Chester Himes reserves the correct title for his hero, who is a novelist like him, black like him, wrecked like him, and insolent like him. Jesse Robinson mulls it over and finds inspiration in his crime. A title occurs to him – the title of a novel that somebody should have the balls to write one day: *The End of a Primitive, the Beginning of a Human*. And this is precisely the novel that its readers are currently holding in their hands. Suddenly everything becomes clear, and we can breathe again, lift our heads a little. Might there be another way? Chester Himes turns the world upside down like a snow globe, and the flakes start to fall on our altered faces.

Jesse becomes tragically aware of his destiny not as a primitive or as a black man but as a human being becoming himself – a primitive evolving into a human. In this closed system, the human being is the civilized white man. A primitive evolving into a human is therefore a barbarian in the process of being integrated, of being assimilated into the Empire. So, when he slaughters his white mistress, Jesse Robinson is not confirming his true inner nature, nor the identity forged by all his frustrations as a rejected black man. What he is confirming is his comprehensive integration into the system. 'Black son of a bitch has got to have some means of joining the human race.'[11] He realizes that what was preventing him from being seen as a human by the ruling white order was precisely the fact that he had morals and principles. In majestic fashion, Chester Himes inverts the conventional hierarchy of values. The white world is the rotten apple that contaminates everything it touches. Non-whites suffer not from being unable to burrow into it like little maggots but from being forced to bite into it and thereby undermining their deeply held values. They are forced into abandoning their souls, for it is the soul that resists integration, not their monsters or their frustrations or their resentments. What resists is their conscience and everything that makes them cling on desperately, for just a little bit longer, to their beauty. 'Reason why you own life was so bitter, son. Had conscience.'[12] The 'regression into savagery' does not therefore arise from a failure to integrate, but from the very process of integrating: 'were a nigger but killed a white woman and became a human being'.[13] In killing this woman, Jesse Robinson makes the great civilizational crime of the white man his own and can therefore lay claim to civilized status. He sells his soul to the Empire and gives himself up to it, just as he gives himself up to the police: 'Went in the back door … a primitive filled with all that crap called principles, integrity, honour, conscience, faith, love, hope, charity and such, and came out the front door a human being, completely purged. End of a primitive; beginning of a human.'[14]

You see the nuance? It's as thin as a cigarette paper – so subtle that it seems constantly to be slipping through our fingers. We need to find a way of holding it steady so that we understand it clearly – so that they understand it clearly.

The regression into savagery is a process of integration. How does this assertion differ from the misguided argument that the violence of barbarians is the havoc wreaked by a racist system? They'll claim we're quibbling over definitions, as they always do when we're trying to affirm our dignity. But the difference is real and significant, and to pretend otherwise is to misunderstand it. Asserting that the *regression into savagery is a process of integration* is not to advance sociological explanations for our inner monsters by tracing the genealogy of all our civilizational shortcomings; rather, it is to state that our monsters are engendered not by too little contact with you but too much – too much France, too much Empire. They are born through contact with you, and it is also through contact with you that they gradually take (self-)destructive shape. That's why you, and all your talk of redeeming indigenous types through integration, can never really save us. In fact, nothing from that world can save us, not only because one thing cannot simultaneously act as the poison and the cure, but because we're not the ones who need saving. It's the familiar story of the sane person in a world of madmen. When the world is sick, the ones that need guiding are not those who resist its laws but all the others. Despite the identity crisis that civilization inflicts on us, ultimately, we are not the ones most deserving of pity. We're pretty good at seizing our opportunities and we're doing alright – but what about them? Imagine just for a few seconds being in the shoes of the heirs of the Empire. All the demons of history would suddenly descend on us. Descendants of Nazis, colonizers, slavers, and genocide perpetrators! 'Whiteness studies' tend to focus on white people's privileges, which is perhaps a little unfair. We should mention too all that they lack – for a start, they seem to lack all those values they still claim to have invented themselves, such as humanism, universalism, democracy, fraternity, and freedom of expression. You can almost understand

the ones who prefer to stand proudly by their crimes
as if it were a question of honour. It's anyone's guess
what's going through their minds ... What Césaire calls
Europe's regression into savagery is not a mere anecdote.

But already I can hear their objections: 'So when
you're ugly, it's a reflection of our ugliness, whereas
when you're beautiful, it's down to your own beauty.
Yeah, right!' In a way, they're correct, and I can't help
smiling at the thought of them taking us literally and
gearing up to defend their honour. They are almost
touching in their insistence, and it's because they're
attached to their beauty too. They don't appreciate that,
for us, this decolonizing ego trip is tantamount to a vital
need. We need it to make us heady with pride, we need
our beauty enhanced and lauded in glowing terms. Our
need to feel proud can never be fully satiated. This story,
though it is somewhat pared back to take into account
what they call 'community sensibilities', is a kind of lie
that tells the truth. We need to let it colonize our brains
because it is the only story capable of competing with
the narratives of the Empire. The only one that can
shine a light for our children and indicate a direction
and a horizon. The only one whose message – neither
wimp nor monster – we should abide by. 'And O my
people, out yonder, hear me, they do not love your neck
unnoosed and straight. So love your neck; put a hand
on it, grace it, stroke it and hold it up.'[15]

The civilized should save themselves the trouble of
fretting about our lot. We are the ones who should be
pitying them, and we are the ones who might be able
to save them. The opposite has never happened in any
shape or form at any time in history. Are there nuances?
Seriously, when were they ever interested in nuances?
When they worked in their favour, obviously. In *Beloved*,

Paul D. has an answer for them. The former slave Sethe describes how a young white girl 'helped her' when she was on the run. Paul D. interrupts and corrects her. Don't ever say that, he says, adding a crucial nuance: *she* was the one who saved the *girl*. When the civilized betray their race to help barbarians, it is their own salvation they are seeking, their own beauty. And my, how fine their beauty is when it appears in that guise; and my, how we admire it and mourn the fate of people such as Fernand Iveton and Maurice Audin.[16] Yes, there exists a story of white dignity, but precisely because it is a question of dignity it shouldn't be paraded around to add nuance to the barbarian narrative of white guilt. Rather, it illuminates the story of the master who has learnt from their slave the higher phase of the dialectic: when it is the slave who teaches the master the meaning of freedom. Not only of the slave's own freedom, which has been arbitrarily taken away, but that of the master too, who is alienated within a relationship that will inevitably lead to mutual destruction. Heaven for all, or hell for all.

Before handing himself in, Jesse Robinson spruces himself up, 'smiling slightly beneath the steady seep of tears'.[17] He is not just crying for himself, his perdition and that of his people. He is crying for white people too, or, more precisely, for all that they are losing. Black beauty, native beauty, barbarian beauty. 'Knew they'd keep fucking around with us until they made us human. They don't know yet what they're doing. Fucking up a good thing. Best thing they ever had for all their social ills.'[18] It's a huge waste that makes you sick to the stomach when you think about it. But, amid Jesse's tears, that goddamn bad-boy smile just won't go away. He can't help himself. Even after calling the cops, who will soon come and throw him in jail, he remains 'half-amused'. The novel ends with that word. Chester Himes wants to 'get the lead out of [our] ass'.[19] All this earnestness and uptightness over the choice of words when it comes to racism is starting to get ridiculous. Over the phone, the guy at police headquarters plays the innocent.

'I'm a nigger.'

There was slight pause before the voice said, 'What's that?'

'Where you been all your life, boy, you don't know what a nigger is?'[20]

They all play the innocent. Talk of races and natives means nothing to them. Words like 'nigger' are double Dutch to them. And confronted with these words, which we have chosen to appropriate so that they never hurt us again, they start sweating and swallow hard. Hey guys, relax, Chester Himes seems to be saying. Sure, one or two may have died, whole peoples and civilizations even, but we can still have a laugh, can't we? And after all, would it really be so bad if this shithole of a world fell apart? Too bad that the whites missed the boat when it came to their own salvation, but did they really deserve saving? On that point, the jury is still out, but the shock value of the ending will never fade: black man kills white woman.

3

The Impossible Community of Tears

'Heaven will avenge us.' As the planes were crashing into the twin towers of the World Trade Center on 11 September 2001, this phrase resounded within me. I had heard it just the evening before from my father's lips. 'Heaven will avenge us', he had said in response to something on the TV news. I can't remember what it was, but I do remember the prophecy, preceded by the words: 'The Americans are the worst thing to have happened on Earth.' The next day, when the attacks happened, it was: 'I told you so!'

It was not an exclamation of pleasure, but rather disbelief: the very heart of the despised fortress had been stormed by a bunch of bearded men armed with kitchen knives. The Axis of Evil had struck the Axis of Good. The black man had once again killed the white woman. My father hadn't *predicted* anything; he'd merely embraced the logic of the world and heard the rumble of what was to come. What happened had been threatening to happen for a very long time, so much so that it was like an over-inflated balloon bursting. To delight in it would have been to side with the enemy, but simple indignation was not an option either. Everything was confused and impossible to get straight. On the one hand, the symbolic power of the American skyscraper conjured up the millions of lives sacrificed with impunity in the building of this Promethean edifice – the ultimate symbol of triumphant modernity, imperialism, and all-powerful capitalism. On the other hand, the unbearable images of those innocent figures hurling themselves into the void to escape from the flames could not decently be reconciled with our usual conceptions of justice. Amid all these confused emotions, we felt lost and concerned for ourselves. Could it be that the injustice of this world had damaged us so much that we were no longer even capable of weeping in the face of such carnage?

Our own consciences were caught in the trap of the Empire, but we had to be given a chance to express what we were really thinking, not just to ward off potentially devastating effects on ourselves but also to salvage something of the contents of our minds. For, in spite of the chasm that our conflicted thoughts threatened to open up in us, they nevertheless captured a certain truth and perhaps even a certain *innocence*. But that truth was drowned out by a hegemonic narrative that dismissed any alternative viewpoint out of hand, before we had even had a chance to formulate it coherently. Those who stood in judgement were unanimous: our failure to shed tears at the sight of these broken lives demonstrated that the evil had been in us from the outset. By failing to join in with the collective outpouring of emotion decreed from on high by the Western powers, we automatically situated ourselves in the camp of the terrorists and their barbarity. Prolonged exposure to this nauseating narrative almost gave it substance. What if we were unconsciously complicit in this horror? The less we were able to express what had gone through our hearts and minds, the more those thoughts and feelings became a source of danger for us. Because the feeling of confusion could not be aired openly, it rotted inside.

Chester Himes's character Jesse Robinson, the black man who killed the white woman, evidently grasped the problem facing our race of barbarians with exceptional acuity, but the insight did him little good. On the contrary, he accepted the monster that the Empire had nurtured within him and he let it take over completely. What are we supposed to do with that? Doom ourselves to the morgue in a war without end? Tell this shitty world to go to hell? The terrorists acted out to a conclusion the destiny that the Empire had reserved for them. At the moment of perpetrating their final act, they had nothing to do any more with us, which is say with that part of us which we have shielded from the assaults of integrationism and remains intact.

They *were* the Empire, its true face revealed in the raw. These monsters – the ghoulish and all-too-familiar embodiments of our regression into savagery – stand opposite another monster whose special power lies in its ability to create the ideological, objective and material conditions that will exonerate it. The incestuous union of the two produced 9/11. On that day, the West experienced an encounter with itself. What did we have to do with all that?

The novel *Invisible Man* by Ralph Ellison opens with a disturbing scene.[1] One evening as the 'invisible man' is walking alone down a poorly lit street, he accidentally knocks into a tall, blond, blue-eyed man who turns around and starts insulting him. Overcome with uncontrollable rage, the invisible man physically attacks him: 'I felt his flesh tear and the blood gush out, and I yelled "Apologize! Apologize!"'[2] When the apologies are not forthcoming, he draws a knife out of his pocket, opens it with his teeth and is poised to cut the man's throat, when at the last second a sudden thought gives him pause.

Recalling his status as an invisible man, he wonders if this man *really* didn't see him and thought he was being beaten up by a ghost 'in the midst of a waking nightmare'.[3] At first ashamed of the crime he was on the verge of committing, he ends up laughing as a new thought occurs to him: 'Would he have awakened at the point of death?'[4]

An avatar of the black man rendered invisible by the denial of his humanity within American society, Ralph Ellison's character has no face and no name. He is not so much an anti-hero as a non-existent hero, both for himself and others. And yet he does exist. How do we know this? On account of all the blows and insults he receives. They are the only palpable proof of his existence. The white man is also an avatar. The black man has already crossed paths with him thousands of times, and the same altercation has taken place over and over again. The black man is suddenly conjured into existence to be on the receiving end of violence and contempt, and once it's over he disappears again until the next humiliation.

'But not this time', Ralph Ellison's invisible man seems to be saying. If he only exists when he's being hit, then he's going to give as good as he gets – the bruised and battered face of his usurper will be the gratifying proof of an existence usually denied to him. It's his way of overcoming his invisibility and raising himself to the status of a man. In the racist system, violence becomes the only means of communicating with others, which is to say imposing a true and equal relationship between two human beings. But in this very act – the final confrontation with his historical oppressors – he seems to experience a revelation. These 'white devils' standing proudly victorious amid their crimes of infamy strike him for the first time as unexpectedly vulnerable.[5] The invisible man stops himself for a second before perpetrating an act of hatred. What he sees lying on the ground is a victim as well as a perpetrator – a victim not merely of a desperate act of vengeance but of an infirmity: a 'moral blindness' which he appears unable to overcome and condemns him to the cruellest of ironies: to be beaten to death by a 'phantom' who does not exist. 'Poor fool, poor blind fool, I thought with sincere compassion.'[6] The tormentor no longer instils fear but pity. The invisible man slashes the air rather than the man because he has an answer, as if from beyond the tomb, to his question: 'Would he have awakened at the point of death?' Watching the prone body devoting its final breaths to uttering further insults, he realizes there are no grounds for hope – the man would have croaked on the asphalt without recovering his sight. The idiot would have died without knowing how or why, like someone dying in their sleep.

Would he have awakened at the point of death? If the question were asked of the victims of terrorist attacks in the West, the answer would be just as final as in the novel: No, they'll never know why they died or what killed them. And all the big talk that follows doesn't help matters. We're lulled by children's stories: good against evil; civilization against barbarity. At that point, we can cry, but we can't *cry together*. For, before the chaos, we were the radical Other for them; we were the ones who were going to drag them down into savagery, orchestrate the Great Replacement and colonize them back. And we're now familiar with the routine, the shift that takes place: what if deep down we were complicit in what has just happened to them? To persuade them that this is not the case, we then do something odd: we remind them that blacks and Arabs were among the victims. Barbarians have been killed by the barbarians. Can't you see that this doesn't make sense? Can't you see our tears are sincere? Actually, we are doing no more than revealing their own mentality: the reason they only believe our tears to be genuine when we're mourning our own is because that is what they do: mourn their own, exclusively. One life in the West is worth how many lives in the South? The community of tears will never materialize because, in a sense, we have more that is *universal* in us than they do, despite all their boasts to the contrary. We carry on our conscience the millions of unmourned deaths precisely because we have failed to mourn them – we are only too aware that the Empire generates victims so that we can all live happily within it, but we've accepted the deal. We've averted our gaze from the shores from which we come. None of those images of the devastation of the South has prevented us from sleeping at night or loving our children. But when the devastation occurs in the West, all our inner conflicts rise to the surface. Why should we cry now, having failed to cry earlier for all the others? So many deaths have gone unmourned, so commonplace have they become, that the Empire has drained us of our tears, and the tank is still empty when it demands that we sympathize with its misfortune. It is something of a challenge to remain consistent and refuse to participate in the collective outpourings of grief, and such a refusal can certainly provoke disgust. But this attitude by no means betrays indifference, and still less a perverse satisfaction. Our torment in fact confirms the extent of our integration, though a certain seditious strain remains in us. Taking to its logical conclusion what the Empire has turned us into, we reluctantly end up confirming the oddness of our position, which is to say barbarians floundering between two poles of barbarity: the Empire and what feels like an inevitable act of revenge. We were *not* all Charlie,[7] partly because of the editorial and political connotations of that slogan, but perhaps above all because it played into the narrative that is trotted out after every Islamist attack – namely that the West has been attacked for what it is: its enlightened values and its zest for life, for dancing, for drinking, and for loving. But what we see is the ugliness of the Empire triumphing and invading us. To echo Ralph Ellison: When will these sleepwalkers finally wake up? What have they allowed themselves to become that they can live so blithely on a heap of ruins? That they can ignore the violence of the world for so long, until it suddenly shatters their lives? That it takes this atrocity, this fateful hour, before they give any serious thought to the ghosts that surround them? Did they really think the two orbits would never intersect? That, by carrying on obliviously with their lives, they would never meet one of those murderous ghosts?

'Heaven will avenge us', said my father, and it was not a prayer. He simply meant that there is a justice associated with every truth on Earth. And this justice did not take the vulgar form of the terrorist attack itself but rather everything that it revealed about this profoundly fouled-up world. 'Heaven will avenge us' was his version of the James Baldwin prophecy encapsulated in the title of his book *The Fire Next Time*, which, similarly, was neither a threat nor a warning but the expression of the permanent state of our inner beauty and the renewed promise to remain this side of the threshold – to risk a fire while at the same time controlling the urge. For this Baldwinian fire within us, which threatens to burn down everything, has to be kept under control without ever being allowed to go out. It has to remain a private barbarian spark that gives us courage for the struggle, sometimes against the fire itself.

4

The Life and Death of Marcelin Deschamps

The uglier we are, the more beautiful they are. The more we go awry, the more we fuel their complacency. We are their evil doppelgangers and they need our corrupt souls to hold onto their innocence.

– Houria Bouteldja[1]

In order to domesticate barbarians, first you need to lecture us about freedom. 'Be free' is the phrase used to draw us into the net, and the thing is, we understand straight away. What *be free* means for us is: free yourself from your own people, their traditions and the archaic practices that ossify them into a homogeneous and opaque bloc. Be free to betray them now that you are under our protection. And everything that we say or do will henceforward meet with the Empire's seal of approval and be credited to the beauty of its world. A new family is reaching out to us that doesn't seem authoritarian in the least. You could almost forget that it even exists – it reigns so serenely over its world that it doesn't feel the need to draw attention to itself. And, in any case, *family* isn't really the preferred word for it, still less *community*. The Empire's acolytes prefer to speak of individuals who have consented to cohere around a set of unchallengeable common values.

Why would we not aspire to be part of that, we who have grown up in a family clan weighed down by a rigid framework of external laws? The barbarian family is an animal forever on its guard. Its nerves are so frayed that it becomes an obsession for everyone to stick together in the face of everything that is conspiring to drive us apart. At which point, the free individuals of the great civilized family will decry our sectarianism, separatism, and indigenism. What they see is a flock of resentful sheep who instantly reach for the word 'traitor' as soon as one of their own tries to find a way out of his or her personal predicament. A flock incapable of using their brains because they're bogged down in ancestral loyalties and too busy fretting about their dignity, which is, in fact, merely a way of concealing the pain of their historic defeat. A flock full of rancour that prefers to stick tightly together in the same shitty situation rather than risk division by negotiating their respective slices of the pie. A flock that ultimately doesn't even trust itself and is thereby already admitting defeat.

People will inevitably see it like that from the outside. But, inside our own homes, we know how flexible this purported community allegiance is. On the doorstep the elders whisper in our ears: 'Go forth, my son, go forth, my daughter, and do what they expect you to do' – but they immediately qualify that by saying: 'Send us signals that you are still one of us, signals that only we will be able to decipher.' Secret telepathy. Every time we stop to take stock, we need to turn around and make sure we haven't gone too far, that we can still see the beloved silhouettes of mum and dad waving, albeit shrinking as we move forward. You need a lot of love to let your kids leave and make their way in a world that despises you, placing unconditional trust in them despite the danger that they will come to despise you in their turn. And those departing need a lot of love to be worthy of this trust – they need to understand that remaining true to one's history is not remembering it through some yellowing photo but realizing its potential in the present. You have to know when to put this history on the line and in so doing cast it in a new form, enriched through contact with the current age.

Does an alarm bell sound when we go too far? Is there a warning signal when betrayal beckons, or is betrayal something we carry with us like a shadow we can never rid ourselves of? Few careers offer a clearer insight into this question than that of Mehdi Meklat, a kid who grew up in a rough suburb and became the darling of fashionable Parisian society, but was then embroiled in a scandal that seriously tarnished his reputation – an umpteenth variation on the classic theme of rising from humble beginnings only for it all to go wrong. There are plenty of others in the French repertoire – Rastignac, Sorel, and Rubempré to name but a few fictional examples – and one would like to add Mehdi Meklat to the roll call, but that would not go down well. In his case, the fallen angel is not merely from humble origins but from the bottom of the pile, from one of France's 'lost territories'.[2] And indeed it is to these origins that he owes both his glory and his downfall.

Mehdi and Badrou (Badroudine Saïd Abdallah) – the inseparable duo, one Arab and the other black, who looked like kids from the deprived *banlieues* (disturbingly reminiscent of a traumatic image that still weighs heavily on the conscience of the nation[3]) – were welcomed with open arms into all the spaces where they should have stood out like a sore thumb: journalism,

37

literature, theatre, TV, and the Élysée. Everywhere they went, patrons of the arts would pat them on the back and boast of their own discernment in having discovered them. Everyone marvelled at these 'ironic and tenacious little elves who will go a long way'.[4] Here were a couple of that kind whom they liked, a couple who spoke their language but also that of the Other. Perfect representatives of *diversity*. In the wake of the 2005 riots, that was the word doing the rounds when people tried to imagine what a miraculous, non-confrontational solution might look like. In order to ease the tensions in the suburbs, one had to consent to listen to them and, amid the profusion of grievances, pick out one that would cost least to appease: visibility in the public arena. In other words, accord them the right to have their own elite – an avant-garde elite from an immigrant background benefiting from positive discrimination, scattered lightly around the editorial departments of the Parisian media. The suburbs had something to say! They were finally going to speak, and we were going to listen. The stakes were huge and a great deal of care had to be taken. The two 'kids' (the English word became their moniker) had to get it right because they *represented* something. Not so much the *banlieues*, in fact, as an idealized version of them concocted by the left, who couldn't get enough of them. Positive and welcoming *banlieues* full of goodwill, and, above all, won over to the progressive cause. *Banlieues* only too willing to contribute to the grandeur of the country with their freshness, vigour, and flow. Let them shake up all the stuffy spaces with their unflinching authenticity because that's exactly the slap in the face the elite needs to reinvigorate itself. And Mehdi Meklat was the perfect man for the job, until this happened:

Bring in Hitler to kill the Jews. #César2012
Long live queers, long live AIDS with Hollande.
Sarkozy = synagogue = Jews = shalom = yes, my son = money. #YouAlsoFinanceTheCampaignOfSarkozy
I miss Bin Laden.
White people, you must die, ASAP.

At the beginning of 2017, 50,000 tweets of this ilk were exhumed from Mehdi Meklat's Twitter account. It was a bloodbath. The 'kid' was thrown under the bus by his benefactors, who wanted nothing more to do with him. It was a sacrifice they had to make to save their world, and was it ultimately such a sacrifice anyway? Had they really known who the guy was? They conducted a postmortem of the deception – surely, behind that image of an inoffensive little rascal, and those polished manners of the miraculous survivor of the suburbs, they should have spotted the lurking beast? They screwed up their eyes looking at old photos and texts – surely there had to be something there that should have alerted them, that they had failed to pick up on? What if he'd been conning them from the get-go? What if he never was that role-model Arab they'd wanted to push as a symbol of successful integration, the 'kid' made to measure to serve the interests of the Pygmalion Left? What if he was … just like the others?

Amid all the public apologies, Mehdi explained that he had created a kind of monster, an evil doppelganger by the name of Marcelin Deschamps, as a virtual safety valve, and that Marcelin was the true author of the hateful tweets. 'I've killed Marcelin Deschamps', he assured everyone.[5]

This is where the story becomes really interesting, but it's also where it finishes. Marcelin Deschamps didn't interest anyone. Mehdi Meklat had to go away and 'take a long hard look at his mistakes and learn from them', as his publisher put it. Learn what, exactly? The lesson the Empire had taken from it was entirely predictable: Mehdi Meklat is a barbarian, a hideous soul who took advantage of the well-meaning naivety and generosity of society to carve out a place for himself that he didn't deserve. Unmasked, he was dispatched back to the limbo from which he came. All's well that ends well?

A year on from his social death, Mehdi Meklat published *Autopsie*, in which he ostensibly sets out some of the lessons he has learnt.[6] In truth, however, he clouds the issue with a hotchpotch of stuff about the dangers of social media, the rashness of youth, and the system being at fault. Although his argument is confused, his intention is clear enough: Mehdi is pawing at the door like a needy cat in a desperate and somewhat pathetic attempt to prove his credentials afresh. It's a shame because, if truth be told, it's Marcelin who makes Mehdi interesting – Marcelin restores to the good-as-gold Mehdi some of the substance and depth that the policy of visibility had stripped him of. But what did Marcelin really stand for? What was the substrate on which this mould grew? The answer is doubtless to be found in the troubling overlap between the ascension of Mehdi and the rise of Marcelin. When Mehdi received praise, Marcelin was all pride and rage. When Mehdi gave thanks to his benefactors, Marcelin spat in their faces. When one smiled, the other screamed. It was in the entrails of integration and amid divided loyalties that the monster was born. Another reading of the situation is therefore possible. Suppose what the benefactors feared was not the threat of Mehdi Meklat morally contaminating their world, but facing up to the realization that it was their world that had contaminated him and enabled the birth of Marcelin Deschamps? How else to explain how such an irreproachably progressive circle could have hosted such an odious monster in its midst? The question didn't seem to occur to anyone. Instead, they rushed to a conclusion: this monster was clearly a foreign body, a virus from elsewhere – in this case, from the *banlieues*. 'We need to purge, clean out, scrape clean', suggested the politician Christiane Taubira, who came in for criticism for having appeared on a magazine cover with the unsavoury duo just a few days before the scandal broke.[7] She evidently thought the issue deserved more than a mere statement distancing herself from him, which is what everyone else was churning out. But did it not occur to her for one moment that this hygienic enterprise she was proposing as a remedy for the regression into savagery should perhaps be applied to the *fashionable society* that Mehdi had joined? Clearly not, for what she was implying was that Mehdi's foul outbursts were of a piece with the engrained filth of his origins, and that the process of integrating him, of civilizing him, must continue in order to *wash off* the remaining traces of his barbarism. 'I confirmed the image they had of me: a kid called Mehdi was inevitably antisemitic and homophobic in their eyes.'[8]

But what if it was the other way round? What if Marcelin Deschamps was not merely the regrettable provocative urge of a *banlieues* kid who still needed to be educated – in other words, a symptom of incomplete integration? What if Marcelin rather than Mehdi was the Empire's true kid, no sooner born than disowned? The very choice of name is actually a clever touch: 'The paradox being that with Marcelin Deschamps, I was above all French, a pure-bred Frenchman.'[9]

Mehdi knew deep down that he was the good conscience of his new friends. Their compliments and kindly smiles ended up making him want to puke. 'I didn't want to please those people, I didn't want to entertain them, ... I wrote the tweets as a reaction to that, to say I'm not like you, in fact I'm against you.'[10] People on the other side of the symbolic divide were also starting to say that he'd changed and was now one of them: 'Some already had the impression that [the radio station] France Inter was infantilizing and manipulating us, and perhaps that was what sowed the first grain of confusion in me.'[11] How to escape from the former while reassuring the latter? The answer was to invent an individual who could erase once and for all the distinction 'between the person moving in beautiful circles with the appropriate smile on his face and this other person who wants to reassure his own people that he has not betrayed them, who wants to scream at his adopted milieu: you see, I'm not like you, I can also say some terrible things, I can press where it hurts'.[12]

It's no coincidence that Marcelin Deschamps's scatological urges were directed at all the categories cherished by Western liberals: gays, Jews, women, and even blacks and Arabs (the ensuing media circus made no mention of these latter categories). What he was attacking was the immaculate storefront, the unbearable innocence of the world that had given him its blessing. Anti-racism, feminism, the LGBT+ cause – that's where he wanted to 'hurt' them. Mehdi as Marcelin was saying to them: Just look at the true face of your progeny, look at the ugliness you believe you are saving the barbarians of this country from but which, in fact, you yourselves are responsible for. 'Both *Marcelin Deschamps* and Mehdi Meklat are the pure product of this society: educated in the values of the French Republic but a terror on Twitter, *good* and *evil*. Both were certified "blue-white-red" because they had antisemitic, misogynist and racist tendencies as well as a dark, typically French sense of humour, all of which involves targeting women, Jews, blacks, Muslims, gays and poor people.'[13] When he says he wants to 'reassure his own people', which is to say the blacks and Arabs of this country, his message is not that we are indeed the regressive (homophobic, antisemitic, and sexist) savages we are imagined to be, or even that we are not those things at all (twisting to our advantage the black box of fantasies about us). What makes his story of the evil doppelganger really interesting is that it allows a dialectical interpretation of the regression into savagery. If we want to find out how progressive liberal ideals are viewed in the *banlieues*, we just have to stop and ask people in the street. And the answer that comes back is that it is a massive exercise in hypocrisy by the powers that be, who parade their best side in order to extend their supposedly civilizing influence. The fact that all these fine ideas are proffered by the same hand that holds under the water the heads of those who inhabit the *banlieues* is bound to influence how they are received. If they are seemingly rejected wholesale, it's not so much for what they are but because they serve in practice to denote the moral superiority of a world that despises them. In practice, progressive ideals on the housing estates are dished out by the police, and in the countries of the South it's frankly via bombs. It's not hard to imagine what a devastating impact such a civilizing mission is going to have on the communities targeted, which makes you wonder if the stated objective is the true one. It's almost as if these modern missionaries are relieved that it's not working – did they really expect it to? What's certainly true is that they are attached to their 'moral high ground'.[14] What they call the 'regression into savagery' is not merely our reaction to their victory – it constitutes the very essence of their victory. In the face of their sheer tenacity, not only do we end up mistrusting them, but we deploy as barricades the purported faults of which they would cleanse us. We create our own inner Marcelin Deschamps to resist the powers that be at all costs, even if this entails a certain moral impoverishment. In a sense, Marcelin prefigures the impending disaster as we become the Empire's evil doppelgangers. Soon there will be nothing left of us. All that will remain is what they've turned us into – what we've become while floundering around in the moral impasse that Western civilization has herded us into.

At the end of *Autopsie*, Mehdi has a vision. He thinks back to a memorable evening a fortnight before the scandal in the recording studio of a leading radio station, surrounded by some of his favourite people: a new generation of artists, writers, and journalists 'from every background'. They represent a new dawn breaking over the old world, and they make a promise to themselves: 'disaster detests groups'.[15] They are an elite, admittedly, but an alternative elite on a mission of emancipation. Looking at them, you'd think you were reading Sartre's preface to *The Wretched of the Earth*: 'The fire that warms and enlightens them is not yours.'[16]

Two years on from the scandal, the disaster has come to pass, and Mehdi Meklat is toxic. That old clique is no more, his sterling brother-in-arms Badrou being one of the few to stand by him. Most of the others have simply vanished into thin air. Gone AWOL. Rumour has it that a crisis meeting was held amid all the turmoil to try and save brother Mehdi, but it soon broke up when its true purpose became clear, namely, to save everyone else *from* Mehdi. They asked him to grovel and assume sole public responsibility. 'Mehdi, please, give an interview on France 2 ... Tell them I had nothing to do with your tweets, I'm begging you. You have to save us, you have to think of us,' implored a star presenter.[17] It was as if Mehdi was seeing his real self for the first time. Adieu, old friend. Carry on clowning about, but don't give me that. Your 'us' is not an us, it's a fragmented me. They thought they were firmly united, but they were not allowed to forget their sorry condition: even after reaching the rarefied heights of society, they proved to be incapable of tilting the balance of power in their favour. Each of them was conscious of the fragility of their position – yet this awareness did not result in solidarity, as they pretended to believe, but in a new social persona that was not compatible with defending the dignity of the world they had in common. While certain individuals might have secured privileges, the collective misfortune persisted.

'We were always sensitive to endings. We always wanted to stage the ending,' confesses Mehdi Meklat at the end of his story, and you have to recognize his talent in that respect, even if he only acknowledges it after the event.[18] There is something Freudian in his downfall, as if it were premeditated. It's likely that we create monsters to punish ourselves for an ambition that we refuse to admit is harming us more than it is elevating us. The higher Mehdi climbed, the deeper Marcelin dug the abyss into which he would eventually fall. It was as if he prevented himself from going too far by devising in advance his own self-destruct button. If the principle of remaining true to your origins is a guiding ideal that

45

gives the upwardly mobile the impression of remaining in control of their destiny, then Marcelin Deschamps can be seen as the punished god of our race.

'Ultimately, this controversy probably had to happen so that I could learn to live with myself and express this truth in writing.'[19] Mehdi Meklat is currently being reborn from his own ashes as part of a new anti-racist scene that happily blurs the boundaries between political engagement and entertainment, but it is not difficult to imagine the ghost of Marcelin observing him from afar ... with a distinct smirk.

5

Ounga Ounga

The lady judge asked, 'Why you do that?'
Ounga ounga ounga, ounga
Dough, moola, bread,
That's why, madre puta.

– Booba, 'Nougat'[1]

'In front of the teachers, I'd pull faces as I dragged on my spliff, coz they told me in class Man comes from monkeys.'[2] It's an archetypal scene: the unruly class dunce on the back row, smirking at the hapless teacher incapable of maintaining discipline. And the recurring complaint: we just don't know what to do with that kid.

Booba is that kid, who has frustrated every effort to tame him, even by the most accommodating domesticators, who thought they were being clever in granting him a little place in their expanded pantheon. Booba, they said, would be a genius of French literature. The Artaud of modern times. The Céline of the street. The filthy tongue that would give the French language a desperately needed shot in the arm. Even the prestigious *Nouvelle Revue Française* endorsed this general view.[3]

Linguists delighted in the article by the writer Thomas Ravier, who coined the word *métagore* to denote a kind of non-literal language invented by the wayward rapper: 'a toxic apparition on the retina, sudden, brutal, impossible to get out of your head: something has registered in your vision'.[4] They thought they'd classified their specimen – he lay there dissected before them, perfectly circumscribed. It was a kind of consecration. The response of the interested party? 'Go fuck yourself, you and your books.'[5]

If that doesn't make you laugh, you really don't get it. Booba is not replying to them directly, but this provocative line encapsulates the stance he has adopted for decades now: a categorical refusal to be seduced by the system. For him, that's the joy – the glee – of writing, though, beneath all the amusement, there's a deadly serious intent. Booba's mission is not just to taunt fashionable society – he wants to pillage and contaminate it. His career plan is crystal clear: to achieve success without being brought to heel. To succeed as a barbarian, as a pirate. They can keep their Pantheon for themselves; he will construct his own, in his own image, but never on terra firma, for the pirate's place is at sea.

'In the 92 pissed off easy, coz whipped in Mississippi'[6]

In reality, Booba is a fiction invented from scratch by one Élie Yaffa, a young Franco-Senegalese man brought up by a white mother on a quiet housing estate in Meudon, just west of Paris. At primary school, he was a quiet and rather conscientious pupil who readily obeyed the teacher's instructions. In the class photo, there's no hint of the future bad boy but there's one thing you do notice: he's the only black child amid all the white kids. That's where the attempts to define him began.

It all began in the playground, their recreation:
Malabar, Choco BN, 'dirty black!', my generation.[7]

Growing 'like a nettle among the roses', he felt he stuck
out like a sore thumb.[8] There had been a screw-up before
he was born which now weighed heavily on his young
shoulders: it was the weight of his race, the colour of his
skin. He was a 'dirty black' at teatime with no partner in
crime to help him give as good as he got. He therefore
had to draw on all the force of his roots to alleviate
his circumstances, all the force of a continent to hold
his own with these budding racists. He was isolated by
this uprooting, which he himself never went through
but which he experienced viscerally. What was he supposed to do? Grin and bear it? Become an exemplary
little black boy, soaking up the insults and trying twice
as hard to earn the respect he deserved? Élie Yaffa's life
could have played out like that, but, when he was ten,
he visited his father's homeland of Senegal for the first
time. During his stay, he went to the island of Gorée, a
hub of the slave trade for more than two centuries, and
imagined himself in the cells, imagined the newborns
snatched from their parents, the women raped, the men
tortured, the bodies sorted like cattle and chained. The
images floored him and lodged themselves in his mind
forever:

Hanged black man passing through my pupils,
Slave blood suckled at the nipples.[9]

This is more than a figure of speech (Ravier's 'non-literal
language') – it's an expression of his rapport with the
world. Something had been sown in him. Anger? Rage?
We had to wait a few years before we could admire the

49

fruits, but, at the age of seventeen, he discovered his talent for rap and everything could finally explode above the surface. Everything could finally be said. This rebirth called for a new name, and he chose Booba, in reference to a cousin of his in Senegal called Boubacar. The intent was barely concealed: Booba would be a force hailing from Africa, a black hero who had returned to avenge his ancestors. 'Become what you are' goes the tired old adage. With Booba, Élie Yaffa sets himself an altogether more interesting challenge: he becomes *what he should have been* – without the original tragedy when the West came crashing into native territories.

Booba intends to be the West's worst nightmare: at once the embodiment and the repudiation of its racist fantasies. His body sculpted like a coat of armour, he will be a delinquent, dealer, killer, and animal. He will be a figure of the evil they've created who has come to settle the score and complete the circle.

> My people whacked,
> It's just temporary,
> 'Til West Indies and Africa fight back.[10]

Paradoxically, it is his experiences as a young black boy destined for integration, and disconnected from his land and community, that enable him to be so radical. He wants to avenge his uprooting and piece his history back together. That's where his fundamentally reckless attitude stems from; and projecting that insolent, naughty-schoolboy façade, he gives the impression that nothing can touch him. He thereby embodies a parallel narrative to the seemingly inevitable fate of people from an immigrant background: their pre-ordained domestication, which eternally perpetuates a brooding self-hatred. Not a hatred of our origins but a deeply buried, barely conscious hatred of the altered, subservient, absurdly eager-to-please individuals that we become under the pressure to conform to a hostile world. There's a truth here whose force we should acknowledge: the only source of shame for a non-white in this world of whites is to conduct ourselves in a supposedly exemplary fashion (and the rewards for doing so are, in any case, dubious). Our shame, like our vigilance, should be directed here, at what we are becoming. It should be understood not in terms of our devalued or stigmatized origins but in relation to our present condition, which is that of being integrated. The shame lies in succumbing to the sirens of the Empire, in imagining that we can get out of our predicament without leaving behind something that is more precious than what we hope to gain. We remain a long way from the serene reconciliation with ourselves advocated by many postcolonial thinkers. With Booba, it's not about making peace with yourself but, on the contrary, abandoning the desire for serenity and reconciliation, which is always a delusion – a surrender dressed up as a virtue. He hammers his creed into your skull: you have to stay out at sea, at war, for 'the piracy is never over' and the white flag 'is always in the wash'.[11]

A strategic regression into savagery

It would appear that certain indigenous peoples have deliberately invented their own character faults. Fully aware of what they were doing, they listened in on what the colonizers were saying about them and then scrupulously parodied the claims being made. The

Jivaroans, 'a combination of wild forces like waterfalls and ravines, like the claws of big cats and the poison of snakes', stunned anthropologists from the civilized world by announcing their terrible reputation was well deserved.[12] A bunch of cannibals and headshrinkers is what we are, they told the invaders in no uncertain terms, who got the message loud and clear: keep off our land or we'll gobble you up! Colonizers and missionaries simply had to accept the fact that in these climes blighted by the most naked savagery, civilization would never take hold.

Through his symbolic regression into savagery, Booba belongs, in a sense, to this tradition, introducing an intellectual and dialectical dimension that is deeper than a simple rejection of the notion that suburb-dwellers have regressed on account of their intrinsic badness. He may delight in the scandal-provoking opportunities of being a bad boy, but it is also a means of activating a mindset of resistance. Indeed, it is the birth of an emancipatory mythology that summons up from the void a whole interior world originating from the margins of the Empire, and this is one of the most striking features of Booba's rap music (and even of rap in general): the faculty for creating original combinations and producing works that contain such strikingly disparate elements. Not conforming to any music theory or repertoire, it is pure experimental power from the bottom up, which includes the ability to incorporate. Its practitioners throw everything into the mix with no respect for the symbolic frontiers that mark different cultural worlds off from each other and rank them in a hierarchy. They'll talk about Dragon Ball Z, God, their mother, fast cars, love, and big buttocks. Some see this as a flippant mishmash of references driven by purely commercial concerns. All this subculture shit in which contemporary rap deals, they say, is a corruption of the genre, which, these days, is about mere entertainment, whereas once it embodied a noble spirit of protest. 'So what?', its practitioners might retort. Is rap the only art form that has to worry about compromising itself by raking in the money? In truth, it's the only one that fully acknowledges that dimension and does not seek to wash its hands of the triviality of the world. On the contrary, rap emerges from the turbulent chaos of the age and makes a point of trying to remain at the centre of it all, seeking images, words, and gestures to capture all the disruptive sensations and menacing underground impulses. The structure of what we call a *myth* functions in the same way: a kaleidoscope that sources its light from all the disparate cultural domains of a society and transforms them – therein lies its magic – into compatible and equivalent elements of a remarkably coherent whole.

Is this why rap seems to have become the ideal space for myths and legends to be reactivated through the prism of our barbaric experiences? Even rap's fiercest critics would have to admit that it's the source of the most epic tales of what it means to be black or Arab in France today. They become pirates, UFOs, shadow warriors, fugitives from the Matrix, or Saiyans with unlimited powers. 'Augmented' by these mythical tales, the barbarians take their place in the history of the world – they break into it, but through the front door.[13] They increase in amplitude and become barbarians in the Homeric sense of the term: an impenetrable power from the limbo of civilization that exercises a fascination so difficult to contain that the civilized always seem to hide away when they see them coming too close. In so doing, the barbarians learn how to see and know themselves other than via the little keyhole through which the social scientists seek to observe them. How do we tell our story in a world that shrinks us? By enlarging ourselves to such an extent that it becomes impossible to encompass us with a single gaze, even if it's well-meaning (*particularly* if it's well-meaning). Rap has forged a magnifying glass. Through it we discover a truth that a life of humiliations could almost make us forget: everything within us engenders a world. And this inner richness, infinite and unexplored, is not the stuff of a mere chapter – it's material enough for an entire book.

'Still dream of recovering my gold'[14]

Booba weaves his narrative around an obsession: recovering the treasure on which this civilization is built. It's a stolen and usurped treasure that needs to be taken back, but you can't put a value on it. It is an almost metaphysical desire for revenge, a wild vision of what emancipation might look like rather than a surrender to the dictates of consumerism. If money only belongs to the powerful, you're hardly selling out by wanting a slice of the action yourself. On the contrary, wealth affords an opportunity to express every facet of your personality, assert yourself in your own distinct way, and confound the social expectations that weigh on you. And the desire is insatiable because it's partly motivated by a need for reparation.

> Unbowed, I make moola with loads to spare,
> Coz I wanna see this country in its underwear.[15]

Becoming what we should have been, thanks, in part, to the power that money brings, is the thought experiment that Booba is inviting us to participate in. It's as if he were saying to us: this is what we'd be saying if we lived in material comfort, if we weren't caught up in a network of vested interests that prevents us from existing outside the civilizing gaze, to which we are shackled in very concrete ways. What would our lives look like without these chains? The thought experiment leaves you feeling elated. Booba gives us a vicarious glimpse into what it is like to feel liberated and shows us how strong, vibrant, and brilliant we would be if we told them a few home truths.

And if it resonates with us to this degree, aren't we entitled to ask whether Booba is in fact us? The *true* us, concealed like a secret while we outwardly spend the best part of our time chasing after paltry rewards. We keep trotting out the same refrain: we just want to be French like the rest of you, and be allowed to blend into the uniform mass. Just forget us; stop talking about us. It's a wish to disappear. But what if a new path suddenly came into view on the horizon? What if a pirate beckoned to us to follow him out to sea, where it becomes possible to express the political potential we are deprived of on terra firma? What would we actually say then? What would we want? It's like an incursion into our inner *maquis*. What does the boldness to be ourselves really mean?

It's important to be clear: what we're talking about here is not a process of catharsis through rap. It's not simply about bringing repressed fury to the surface, all the better to channel it. Booba's rap captures a barbaric consciousness in a language specially tailored to this end. A 'toxic apparition on the retina, sudden, brutal, impossible to get out of your head: something has registered in your vision', in Thomas Ravier's words. To which we should add: something has been *made possible.*

And our point of entry into the 'language of rap' should be right there: we should consider it as a *roughing up* of language, rather than some sort of enrichment or reinvigoration of the language through contact with recently arrived foreign communities. With all due respect to the linguists and French professors who get all worked up about a zeugma or chiasmus they have cleverly detected in a couplet, the result of their endeavours is always the same: a whole lot of nothing. When you shine an academic spotlight on rap, it goes missing in action. Where it goes, and how it might be persuaded back, is anyone's guess. But everyone can immediately feel that this very powerful thing has been reduced to a damp squib by being dissected like that. Rap is an explosion on the horizon. You can contemplate the scale of the destruction, but you always arrive after the event.

What rap does to language

'I'll fuck France until she loves me.'[16] That line's not from Booba, but it's the very essence of a good punchline: a verbal sally that hits us between the eyes and leaves us a bit stunned. What's going on here? We take on board the meaning: fucking France is already quite an undertaking. But the 'until she loves me' is beyond the pale, inevitably conjuring up the image of a woman who ends up enjoying being raped. Confronted by such violence, we hastily start interpreting. Is this the expression of a boundless hatred for France, or is it on the contrary a cry of unrequited love that betrays a desperate desire to be loved by her? And so we trot out the textual exegesis: might the personification of France as a raped woman be a deliberate reworking of that archaic, and ambivalent, racist fantasy of the savage *banlieue*-dweller raping the civilized woman? Ah yes, well spotted! We pretend we're satisfied with that, but actually we're a bit disappointed. Is that all it amounts to? That extraordinary violence – power? – which left us stunned was just a well-crafted metaphor, a few cleverly chosen words? We sense we're missing something, that we've once again arrived after the event – *after* the rap track, *after* the attack, reduced to sifting through the scattered shards of language to try and reconstruct what has happened. But if we want to capture *what makes rap what it is*, we have to return to the *exact moment of lift-off* when we let out a 'yuck!' and make a 'no' sign with our hand. Rap is really not about semantics. The question is not 'how is rap written?' but 'what *happens* in rap?'. That's where we need to seek its essence.

'Fuck France until she loves me': is that what rap *does* to language? In other words, it not only *debases* it (which people often imagine is the only avenue open to subversive writing); it turns it into something *alien*. From this perspective, when it comes into contact with rap, language is no longer merely language, no longer merely words – it becomes something Other. Its opposite? Provided we appreciate that the opposite of language is not silence but the event. Returning to the question 'what *happens* in rap?', we could now try rephrasing it: what if rap *makes language happen*? Isn't this in fact what people are trying to express through the endless series of nouns (clash, game, punch) applied to rap to describe its effects? It's as if a word is brought to life – resurrected from the cemetery of standard every-day language – to stamp its imprint on matter, and once it has been intoned, it vanishes again. Linguists can pick over it if they like, but it's now dead matter. Rap has released its power into the air, and that power isn't stabilized anywhere, in any sign or language. It's in the flow, that very distinctive way of arranging and reeling off words like a flurry of slaps in the face. That's where the punchline lies – never in the bare text itself. If you analyse it in abstraction like a literary quotation, you can make it mean anything. But if you resituate it within the whole, it will regain its vitality and, once again, offer up a myriad of unexpected meanings. Something is renewed, though it is never possible to fix it firm (and certainly not for the purposes of analysis). Rap exists only when experienced and understood as an event, which is to say when it exits from language. Or, to put it more bluntly, when it destroys language.

And so the linguists hand over the baton. If rap resists a linguistic analysis, then let it stand in the witness box and state its project. 'What are they trying to express?', ask the sociologists, intrigued by the notion of the *banlieue*-dwellers hesitatingly expressing a half-formed message in rudimentary language. Is it a protest? A demonstration? Speak, and we will translate for you. They're forever trying to translate, as if incapable of accepting something for what it is. Rappers rap – isn't that enough? Apparently not. For society only seems to consider rap legitimate when it claims to be deliver-ing a message. Rap is supposed to bear witness and, in so doing, to cater to expectations. When ejected out of its natural orbit so that it can be examined, it once again slips through the fingers. It won't kowtow to the

well-meaning intentions of society. But what about politically engaged rap, you might retort? All those tracks
aimed at the powers that be? We shouldn't get carried
away by appearances. Rap is often not looking to be
noticed beyond its own ecosystem. It's not seeking any
external justification; it's just doing its own thing.

Suffering souls will have to console themselves
elsewhere. Rap, and especially Booba's brand of it, is
not trying to tell society anything. If it did, it would
somehow be bringing itself back into the linguistic fold
of the Empire. Instead, what is driving it is an urge to
undermine everything that is expected of it. We spoke
of 'destroying' language. Who's worried at this pros-
pect, and who's amused? We can identify this as the
first line of demarcation, though we need to be clear:
a language cannot completely destroy itself. But what
can be sabotaged is its pretension to reflect a common
identity. The French language is particularly inclined
to this, even when it is supposedly opening itself up. It
will happily demarcate a little linguistic ghetto within
its territory – in literature, this goes by the name of the
'Francophonie'. But rap knows how to parry this ruse.
The euphoria comes from there: burning down – as a
harraga – the symbolic boundaries that dictate language
use. And, in so doing, it is riding roughshod over the
very idea of the French language reflecting a common
identity. It is resisting the domination that French seeks,
through the classroom, to exercise over all the other
languages that it holds in such contempt; it is resisting its
(totalitarian) pretensions to having universal reach. And
it's hardly surprising that this approach should be largely
restricted in this country to the *corps d'exception*.[17] An
embodiment of the unassimilated foreigner, the *banlieue*-
dwelling rapper is a literal barbarian: he possesses no

language of his own, and the language he borrows (or, rather, the one that history has imposed on him) passes through his lips like an illegal alien, liberated from the rules that have been drummed into him. It has become a hybrid form through contact with other languages and seedy streets occupied by more recalcitrant, less exemplary types. It has *polluted itself* and at the same time *cleansed itself* of the civilizing ambitions of society. Rap reproduces within language the tragedy of exile. It uproots words from their original context, displaces them, and mistreats them. It breaks their attachments, but, at the same time, it emancipates them. Taken out of their comfort zone, words find unexpected inner reserves and are born afresh. They themselves become *harragas*. This is the privilege of the dispossessed: to perceive better than anyone else the potential of a language that overfamiliarity and servility have prevented others from imagining. It's no longer merely an aesthetic affair, though neither is it more political (in the mundane sense of anti-establishment). Rap is also an ethical affair that has this to say: the French language is a temple just waiting to be destroyed by those who were stopped and searched at the entrance. The walls that it has so carefully erected are already trembling under their repeated assaults, and it's just possible those walls will ultimately cave in.

It's a permanent clash, an art of warfare. It's the movement of the sea, eternal and unassailable; the *maquis* of the pirates where the laws of the mainland are suspended and where states themselves struggle to control their borders. It's the place where everything is possible. The storyteller is saying that we are losers here on land, but off the coast a mental horizon is taking shape. Are we going to continue to scratch out a living – a few scraps of civilized land – or are we going to rally to the Jolly Roger? Disillusioned the resistance may be, but it is also re-energized by the sheer panache and pride of the pirates. Should we negotiate our slice of the action or work tirelessly to translate the pirate legend into a political reality? The outcome would be unpredictable, to say the least, but this political fiction at least has the merit of reinjecting some vitality into the enterprise. *Become what we should have been*: a maxim that evokes the dizzying ocean depths where it becomes possible to rediscover ourselves – or lose ourselves forever.

Let's solider on, flag flying and cannons firing,
Don't weep, bro, we'll meet again in the ocean deep.[18]

6

Fucked for Life

I grew up in the zoo, I'm fucked for life.
Even if I die on the beach, I'm fucked for life.
Coz those I luv feel hate, I'm fucked for life.
Coz I run after dough, I'm fucked for life.
– PNL, 'Zoulou tchaing'[1]

In the twilight days following the Paris terrorist attacks in 2015, the country was in sombre mood and all eyes were turned to the *banlieues* – the cursed place from where young men full of hate had emerged and, in one fell swoop, had made the transition from petty crime to bloodthirsty barbarity. People had mental images of squalid abodes on an Aubervilliers housing estate just north of Paris, occupied by dodgy types in tracksuits vacillating between crime and Islam, brooding over their misfortunes and completely alienated from society. The curious physiognomy of a two-headed monster was conjured up in everybody's mind. Chérif and Saïd Kouachi, Brahim and Salah Abdelslam – on each occasion, it was two brothers preaching their sermon of hatred. At the same time, in this same country, an important musical phenomenon was coming into being and spreading at a remarkable speed: the duo of Tarik and Nabil, two brothers from a housing estate in the southern-Paris suburb of Corbeil-Essonnes, who, by their own admission, were brimming with hate. The story of the PNL rap duo began in an atmosphere of catastrophe.

PNL came out of suburbs that were cut off from the rest of the world, a suburban zoo that felt like an extension of prison. An ecosystem had grown up in its heart with its own codes and its own language. PNL's oeuvre comes from there, though 'comes' is perhaps not the right word because it doesn't take a single step towards the outside world. It's proud and dismissive. It stakes out its territory from the get-go: QLF (*que la famille*).[2] In other words, be on your way if you're not one of us, because you just won't get it. Lyrically, phonetically, musically, it will all be unintelligible and perhaps even ridiculous to you. Don't waste your time. This world's not meant for you and no one can explain it to you because these things are not conveyed through expounding but through belonging to the group, through *blood* ties. Too bad for dialogue. The PNL *banlieue* doesn't do socially aware rap, doesn't take issue with any institution, and doesn't raise awareness. It no longer expects anything from the outside world, and doesn't have anything to say to it. Something has broken, but it's too late to talk it over. No interviews will be granted, no 'featuring' collaborations. The fewer we are, the better. It's 'save your own, not save your own skin'.[3]

Who could have predicted that this brazen sectarianism would chime so well with the zeitgeist, spawning on every housing estate in France an army of PNL lookalikes with their improbable slicked-back hair, tight jeans, and crudely printed T-shirts? It hardly matters whether it was a touch of genius or just good marketing. Either way, PNL carved out for themselves an immediately recognizable space. It's the grand tale of the margins of the Empire and their dark side, the shadowy figures in the lobbies of tower blocks, the dope dealers, the lookouts, the electronic tags, and the 'thousand euros in reserve'.[4] But that's just the backdrop. What's striking is the intimacy: this is an inside story of *hess*, so intimate that you sometimes feel embarrassed and wonder if rap should be so open, or whether you're entering a different realm.[5] This monstrous creation is the product of a conundrum: how do you tell your story so intimately when you're in the lion's den and any wrong move can be your undoing? For PNL to tell their story in hostile territory, the first thing they had to do was fence off a space for expression that signals their complete intransigence and a fundamental break with the enemy. To demarcate this space, they have their famous QLF, but they also appropriate the lexical field of savagery. The motif is deliberately chosen to evoke the old colonial division: barbarity versus civilization, savagery versus Empire.

> Homie, I'm a savage and I yell ounga wawa, ounga ounga, gun pointed at the snitch
> Ounga ounga, nigga wawawawa, ounga ounga, so long as we don't cause no havoc
> I know I ain't integrated, I'm boss of my fate
> My hands deep in shit whereas they was made to obliterate.[6]

They begin by depicting themselves as coarse prototypes, as Darwinism gone awry, railing against the open-air zoo in which they live. Sticking with the animal metaphors, they describe a conscious and deliberate moral regression: 'I wanna be empty, soulless, become an animal again.'[7] But this gradual withering away of their humanity does not have the expected effect of reducing them to mere brutes, counteracted, as it is, by an opposing narrative of overwhelming sensibility and even fragility. It's suddenly as if everything is opening up to us. PNL take the familiar stereotype of the dodgy-looking young dealer skulking around in the shadows and open up his entrails so that we can have a good look inside. We're not by his side but *inside* him, and we can feel everything: the wandering about in the dark forever on the lookout, the police patrols, the customers arriving and leaving, the thwarting of love in a world without women.

> Went up on the roof and welled up
> Alone with my thoughts, I'll fuck the world.
> ...
> I love ya, I love ya, I love ya
> I dream of erasing your scars,
> And to save the whole world,
> I wouldn't give an ounce of your life.[8]

This uninhibited display of melancholy, these declarations of love for a revered father, this profusion of tears shared with the moon – it all provokes a kind of aesthetic dissonance. Chest puffed out to bursting, the brute ends up crying. But what really prompts this sense of excessive intimacy is not so much the feelings that are laid bare as the overlapping of two spheres of existence that you would have thought were mutually exclusive: being a barbarian and being a sensitive individual. And here we touch on the heart of the project: telling your story as a barbarian, paradoxically, becomes a way of telling your story as a human being without resorting to the well-meaning clichés of civilization or pandering to its perverse fascination with poverty and misery.

FUCKED FOR LIFE

Their name is already a clue: PNL is an acronym for
'Peace and lovés'.⁹ They ironically evoke the old hippie
slogan only to subvert it, that acute accent and the s
warding off any hint of sentimentality and pitching them
squarely back into their roguish reality. They cannot
risk showing fragility for fear of losing their credibility
in the zoo – but at the same time, they resist what the
zoo is pushing them into becoming by creating a space
where they can finally express their humanity without
making themselves vulnerable in the eyes of the Empire
or suspect in the eyes of their own. They are 'fragile like
peace': a neat phrase that can be interpreted either as a
confession of vulnerability or a threat of war.¹⁰ In this
narrative balancing act, a new figure emerges – not the
barbarian but that part of him that is supposed to be
missing, namely his soul. And what might the soul of
a barbarian look like? PNL's answer is that it's a soul
that's been busted up and gone rotten under the colo-
nizing influence of a poison just as strong as the drugs
that condemn them to skulking around in the streets all
day long. And whose fault is that? The zoo's. But that's
no excuse for just moping around there like depressed
animals, and this is the other side of the PNL project.
It's not just the intimate telling of a scoundrel's tale, it's
the hatching of an escape plan.

'I'm the rotten apple that makes
it out of the barrel'¹¹

Ademo and N.O.S., the avatars of Tarik and Nabil
respectively, share the deep conviction that certain
people have to get their hands dirty in order to burnish
the honour of everyone else. Getting out of what they

call the 'zoo' requires martyrs, but they are no heroes. What gives them their mandate is the fact they are already pretty much screwed, already contaminated. In truth, they're a disgrace to their kind: 'drugged-up hoodies' whose own family will no longer open the door to them.[12] Not because the family refuses to let them in, but because they won't even knock at the door. They prefer to remain in the darkness of the landing because they know they're contagious for those they'd like to save from the destiny they've embraced – among them the 'little brother' who so far has been spared from the laws of the zoo. But for how much longer? This little brother doesn't actually exist. In PNL's world, he's a figure who stands for the innocence that persists beneath all the layers of moral impoverishment. This 'remainder of oneself' that remains miraculously untouched by all the filth of this world is their one truly precious possession. The balancing act becomes ever more perilous: they have to embody all the infamy of the world to save their actual family, while at the same time barricading within themselves the allegorical little brother so that he remains intact while they make good their escape, albeit at the price of a diabolical pact:

I've destroyed myself building a future for my own.[13]

'Am I my brother's keeper?', raps Sefyu, adopting as his own Cain's line in the bible, which was also referenced in the 1984 memoir of the African American writer John Edgar Wideman.

I walk and talk like my big brother
I act like my big brother, I shoot like my big brother
I drink and smoke like my big brother

> I do hold-ups like my big brother, fuck about like
>   big brothers
> I walk and talk like my big brother
> Mad like my big brother I shout at my big sister
> I destroy the life chances of my little brother
> Fuck it, am I my brother's keeper?[14]

It's a classic question when it comes to the relationship between brothers: are we responsible for how the lives of our siblings turn out? Whereas, for Sefyu, the curse of the 'life gone awry' is systematically passed on from brother to brother, PNL invite us to look at the vicious circle from a different angle that reconciles delinquent rap with big-brother rap. For them, the big brother's responsibility lies not in setting an example by returning to the straight and narrow. This time, the question (am I my brother's keeper?) is asked from the point of view of the brother gone awry: do I have to wreck myself so that my brother doesn't have to go through all that himself? Do I have to sink to an all-time low so that he can reach a higher moral ground? If there's such a thing as a dialectic of entangled destinies, then these two individuals hanging around down in the lobby really are their brothers' keepers – they're the night watchmen.

> My life, my life
> Why do you lose souls like that?
> This world is hurting and I can feel that
> They're in darkness but I can see them.[15]

The family extends beyond blood ties to a community with a shared destiny to which they feel morally accountable and for which they're willing to sacrifice just about anything. The clan motto 'QLF' becomes a rallying cry for a wider than expected constituency. It is adopted by all the black sheep of the community, who recover some kind of dignity by allocating themselves a crucial role in the general economy of the group.

In the 'Deux Frères' video, a child is woken in the night by a riot outside in the street. It's October 2005 and this child is well aware that he's part of the race of feral children in hoods that the riot police have been ordered to bring under control. This formative experience sets the scene for what follows, the message being: this is where you're going to have to grow up. But, for the generation of the PNL brothers, it's already the end of childhood – the age when the republican myth of everyone being equal is going to shatter, and the real and symbolic frontiers between them and us are going to make themselves felt. The little brothers Zyed and Bouna are dead and there's nothing left to save.

'I find this sorry tale beautiful'[16]

The escape is turning out to be more ambitious than planned and no longer concerns the zoo alone. This is PNL's grand utopia: they need to leave the earth for the moon (that great confidante of the screw-ups of this world) and start to write a new story on its white expanses – the story (which they have been robbed of on earth) where they cease to be the losers. But, over the course of their albums, this story too starts to go awry. The closer they get to the summit, the further the moon seems to recede. It is a point of light that taunts them in the night: 'I clock the moon giving me the finger.'[17]

And yet there was nothing naive about the strategy: 'deep in the hole, I pile up my sins and start climbing'.[18]

They were just mistaken about the direction they were taking. Tracing out a glorious path for guys like them involves aggravating their situation and plunging into the darkness. 'Making dough', the activity around which all their dreams of escape are centred, is more than a mere capitalist dream. It's the practical enactment of an *ascent out of savagery* – a reverse process whereby you get your hands dirty first so that you can get clean later on. And the very telling of this story is performative: it enacts the process of getting clean within the specific environment of the rap world. In hatching their escape plan, PNL are already in the process of breaking out, as they state very explicitly:

I come out with shit words and you pay, pay, pay me.[19]

If you want white people to get off on it, you have to give them the impression they're looking through the spyhole of a door in a tower block – that they're catching a glimpse of the real you. They catch this intimidating scoundrel red-handed in a moment of vulnerability, affording them an opportunity to bestow their kindness and to forgive him for scaring them so much out in the street. They find him almost lovable, in fact. What if we became friends? What if we were QLF too?

Delighted my hate wins you over.
Delighted we're fucking you over.[20]

'We're not like them, not like them, not like them' is the mantra that PNL repeat over and over again like a badge of pride. They see themselves as the eternal delinquents, forever the sons of a bandit: 'My hoodie upbringing stays tattooed, even if I up sticks.'[21] Even at the top of the Eiffel Tower, they're still night watch-men surrounded by tower blocks; even up high, they're forever looking down.[22] And even the moon has lost its appeal: 'Don't like the moon no more, you can have it.'[23] You'd think the only reason they climbed up there was to shove their beautiful misspent lives in our faces – the sort of life we'd all get off on.

To defend the honour of that way of life, they had to be able to leave it behind. Their latest album to date, *Deux Frères*, reads like an epilogue haunted by the memory of the life they no longer lead. The last track, 'La Misère est si belle', reels off a long list of all the ugly aspects of that life: 'my cockroaches', 'my cellar', 'my lobby', 'my sad roof', 'RER C', 'Building C'.[24] They're not looking to recreate their old world by highlighting the elements of it that society would consider beautiful. They're saying that the beauty of their world lay pre-cisely in its ugliness. And they've also experienced the opposite paradox: the beauty of the world at the apex is revolting when seen up close. It has no moral superior-ity over the life they've left behind; in fact, it's a rather suspect beauty. If it has become possible to assert, as per the track title, that 'hardship is so beautiful', this is not the amnesia of the nouveaux riches talking – it's the reactivating of the distant emotions and half-forgotten memories wherein lies the dignity of the parasites of this world. This reconstruction of the past after the event takes the form of a succession of candid images of a mental state. It's an inner collapse that offers a chance to sift through the ruins of the self and salvage what's worth saving.

They've destroyed our towers,
But won't destroy the empire we've built in our
hearts.[25]

This inner empire should, of course, be understood as a fresh variation on Kateb Yacine's 'certain barbarism'. At the end of their relentless charge to the summit, the two brothers ultimately backpedal: from now on, they're deliberately contaminated and incurable. Happily *fucked for life*.

7

The Path of Blame

Something is bound to have struck the reader: the only barbarians here are men, and men described by a woman to boot. It could well be that the whole raison d'être of this book is to avoid falling into a certain pigeon-hole: to avoid writing *as a woman from an immigrant background*.

These days, in progressive circles, writing as a non-white woman functions as an open sesame: the door opens for us before we've even knocked. We're welcomed in, almost as if they were waiting for us. And this is never a good sign, because, whenever we've been well treated in the past, it's been to bring us into the fold. The model pupils among us, those who can be separated from our veils and integrated, have the wherewithal to negotiate our entry. Putting a female spin on the story of integration – the *beurette* against the barbarians – has always been a means of luring us in, of playing on our gender interests at the expense of our men. I'm personally of the view that this special treatment is our scourge – a cursed inheritance that any woman from an immigrant background with writing ambitions now has to contend with. Barely has she picked up a pen than a million souls are looking over her shoulder. How will she manage to avoid all the traps that her situation sets for her? How will she tell her story and get things off her chest without revealing awkward secrets or stepping over the line into obscenity? How will she deflect ill-intentioned gazes, voyeurism, and false compassion? Is it really legitimate to put the words 'as a woman ...' into our mouths? They're no doubt well suited to political meetings, but aren't they too closely associated with Western campaigning initiatives? What does a *woman's perspective* promise? A story scrutinized through the keyhole, recounted from the bedroom? We're expected to offer up the keys to a private world that is normally screened off by the community, male propriety, and veils – intimate and sometimes sordid scenes, with immigrant women playing their age-old role of settling unsavoury disputes.

Faced with such a dilemma, my unfortunate fellow female writers have made a choice: reluctant to act as native informants, but nevertheless willing to tell our stories, we have built museums. And a whole new genre of literature has thus appeared. For those who know how to interpret it, it brings good tidings: we're no longer falling into the trap. There's no longer any chance of turning us into the *tirailleuses* of the Empire or the fervent champions of integration.[1] Instead, we're going to place on the record – and extol the wonderful virtues of – the blue-collar labour of our fathers, the *ghorba* of our parents and grandparents, the trials and tribulations of our brothers and cousins, forgotten cultures, and the Islamic, Berber, and African elements of our uprooted, fantasized, and mythologized identities.[2] We're going to avenge this community which the Empire has scornfully dismissed and at the expense of which it has fraudulently dangled a new future before us.

Our role as archivist or scribe will consist primarily of cleansing our own people of the stigma associated with them, and of going beyond the stereotype. They've been written off as awful, dirty, and nasty, so we'll give them a makeover by telling exactly the opposite story. We'll try not to leave any dodgy or compromising loose ends – everything will indeed be cleaned up. It will be an act of defiance, a way of saying that racism has not destroyed us as you'd been hoping. It has not eaten away at our deep inner belief in our own morality. On the contrary, the more you torment us, the firmer that belief becomes. Henceforward, we are human beings who have been 'augmented' by the ordeal of rejection.[3] The racists were hoping to create monsters, but in fact they only had one to deal with, and it was the most formidable of all: the monster of dignity. This (literary) strategy has a certain nobility, and there is a clear need for it. Non-whites everywhere are demanding to see themselves represented in their most flattering light, and it's difficult to ignore this and not participate in the drive for collective reha-bilitation. There's an urgent need to learn how to love and live with ourselves, which literature is expected to cater to, and so we go along with it. There are so many scores to settle ... but, ultimately, the effect is limited. Everything is clean and tidy, but in seeking to promote our own virtues we've rendered ourselves inoffensive – not augmented but insipid. When the self-examination has a sociological dimension, it's even worse: it's as if we've been *explained*, and no longer hold any secrets for anyone. It's at this point that we become aware of the perverse ingenuity of the trap we thought we had sidestepped. Full of good intentions in wanting to avoid the usual clichés, we've once again become the teacher's pet and handed in the essay expected of us.

What if we're inadvertently resurrecting the figure of the *beurette*? Not, this time, the compliant figure embraced in conservative circles but the welcome critical voice: the pretty native who talks about 'domination' and 'racism' with grace and sophistication. In stead-fastly carrying out our laborious mission as archivists, biographers, photographers, and makers of documen-taries about our own people, we have created icons and heroes. There has been a universalizing spirit behind our endeavours: *everyone* should see how beautiful and courageous we are. And, in a sense, we have suc-ceeded – but at the price of being transformed into objects of consumption. The luxury brands all have their streetwear lines, and rap is the most streamed music in France. The street now shapes all the visual culture of our age. We women from an immigrant background have been, and are being, hijacked – not by the state but by business. How can we fail to notice the way the entertainment industry is glamourizing us and promot-ing us as ambassadors for urban culture because we seem open and attractive, and therefore easier for the general public to identify with? And all that despite the fact that we're being authentic. The problem is that you can't sell your own culture with impunity. This is not a case of cultural appropriation but of cultural *exploita-tion*: we expend crazy amounts of energy raising our profile and trying to blend into the universal. And the universal then feasts on us and spits us straight back out. You get the impression that the more ubiquitous we become, the more we're associated with Nike, Lacoste, and Versace, the better the likes of Zemmour do in the polls.[4] All that energy wasted. The tragedy is that all this hard work gets drowned out. We have nothing to show for it (except a few fat salaries for the lucki-est ones). The non-white female writer cannot prevent herself from being absorbed. The progressive media put together a panel of women from an immigrant background like they would a bouquet of flowers. We see them posing, proud and dignified, on the front cover. They're powerful, and they're shaking the foundations of the Establishment, we're told. Yeah, right.

I've written this book because I've failed – failed to remain a barbarian. I'm a model pupil of the Republic, a good native with straightened hair who expresses herself in domesticated language. Was I also destined to appear on that front-cover photo? Kateb Yacine's phrase gave me a glimpse for the first time of a possible alternative path, but I was still faced with the conundrum of putting a female twist on the remaining-a-barbarian strategy. How to go about spoiling our model-pupil image when the respectability of our families rests to such a large degree on our shoulders, and when our voices constitute a rare opportunity for our community to have a say in the conversation?

In the preceding pages, I have turned to rap as a way out of this dilemma, but isn't there a potential paradox there too? Don't rappers speak badly of women? Indeed, isn't that one of the more obvious markers of their savage nature? But it hasn't been my intention to translate the language of rap into the sort of universalizing discourse that is typical of academia. Rather, I have the feeling that the rappers have spoken *for* me – not about me but for me. Their language, their excesses, and their irreverence for established grammar give my own prose, as a socially integrated woman, a bit of room to breathe. I'm no longer all alone with my museums, my nice photos, and my pretty knick-knacks. How can these barbarians be the spokesmen for us women from an immigrant background? The answer is in the question. In remaining barbarians, they are speaking for me, for us.

That's the intuition behind this book: if rap is the crystallization of something approaching a barbarian ethics, then, as writers, we need to conceive of a literary equivalent that would conserve rap's power and belligerence as we tell our story – a story that extends beyond saintliness, exemplary behaviour, and even beauty. In this respect, rappers are reminiscent of the Malamatis of medieval Islam who took the *path of blame*. Insofar as the ego is the source of all vices, the Malamatis deliberately chose to lay themselves open to blame and to avoid ostentatious piety in order to prevent their egos from swelling. Extremely devout, they pretended not to be: pure of heart, they were contemptible in the eyes of others and according to the conventions and laws of their time. Might rappers, who are often believers, be the Malamatis of today? Plumbing the filthy depths, they bear paradoxical witness to a pent-up saintliness. 'The final judgement will be intense but things'll be better by then,' proclaims Ninho, having 'screamed so much while I prayed: things ain't been right since the slave trade'.[5]

The ethics and above all the aesthetics of remaining a barbarian are doubtless contained in that wisdom: a suspension of judgement, and of mercy. Our saintliness is buried and hidden, but you can't have the pearl without the surrounding shell, however tough, abrasive, and unsightly it might be. We non-white women are not obliged to choose between judging and idealizing. We could no doubt learn to tell our story with the utmost compassion, despite our sometimes tragic destinies. But first, we need to eschew our assigned roles as arbiters of republican values and high priestesses of the entertainment industry. We need to find our own path of blame.

Notes

1. A Certain Barbarism

1 Sony Labou Tansi, *Encre, sueur, salive et sang* (Ink, Sweat, Saliva and Blood), Paris: Le Seuil, 2015, p. 50.
2 Interview with Jean-Marie Serreau, *France Culture*, 23 February 1967. Translator's note [TN]: The 1967 interview was part of the series 'Images et visages du théâtre d'aujourd'hui' on *France Culture*, radiofrance.fr. To give more context to Yacine's phrase, here is a longer citation of the part of the conversation in which it appears:

> There is one side that is, if you will, quite barbaric. I partly reject our culture. It is a serious dilemma to be forced to live, write and cultivate oneself all at the same time. We cannot do all three, especially if we also want to accomplish revolutionary work, and in addition remain free in life, always free, free to see everything, if we want to push things to the end. So, obviously, you have to choose. You have to choose, for example, between going to the theatre every night or going out onto the street and seeing people, or shutting yourself away and writing. I feel I have so much to say that its best I don't become too cultured. I have to keep this kind of barbarism, I have to stay barbaric. It seems easy to do but in fact it's very, very hard, because there is always, especially in a city like Paris, the temptation of cosmopolitanism, the temptation to want to acquire notions of culture that in fact are not essential – that are things one can know, but for those who

really want to create, those who want to attack and destroy, this can hinder them.

3 Harar is the Ethiopian city where Rimbaud went off the radar after giving up writing for good and leaving the Parisian literary scene behind.

4 In Arabic, *kateb* means writer.

5 A reference to his novel *Le Polygone étoilé*, Paris: Le Seuil, 1966.

6 Toni Morrison, *Beloved*, New York: Vintage Classics, 2022, p. 230: 'What *are* these people? You tell me, Jesus. What *are* they?'

7 TN: *Beur*, now a little dated, is a colloquial term denoting second- or third-generation North Africans living in France. The female equivalent, *beurette* (see p. 75), has taken on pejorative overtones. *Blédard* refers to people from a North African background. *Harraga* is an Algerian Arabic word for illegal North African migrants to Europe.

8 Pascale Casanova, *La République mondiale des Lettres*, Paris: Le Seuil, 1999. Pascale Casanova, *The World Republic of Letters*, trans. Malcolm DeBevoise, Cambridge: Harvard University Press, 2004.

9 Labou Tansi, *Encre, sueur, salive et sang*, p. 88.

10 TN: The French for hyphen is *trait d'union* (joining mark), which also conveys a more general sense of a link.

11 Abdelkebir Khatibi, *Tattooed Memory*, trans. Peter Thompson, Paris: L'Harmattan, 2016: 'The token Arab said, "I am a hyphen between Orient and Occident, Christianity and Islam, Africa and Asia," ... Poor Arab, where did you end up, reduced to a series of hyphens! I saw some who went begging for some image of their identity in newspapers and magazines, flocking to the slightest deletion of due recognition. "Go ahead," said the Pharisee, "insult yourselves this way in our language, we'll give you credit for using it so well." The writers I have described in a lousy book of mine – my first love child with the West – wrote like grade school teachers and, on top of everything else, you had to grant them a meager and passing glory in view of the great cause

of the oppressed. Girded in his beard, Sénac, in his actions, imitated the fakir, calling everyone "brother." Others tortured their pens in this cause: folklore stories, as a minimum to hide in, and at the other extreme the hallucinations of the split person who was no longer sure of the sex of his parents.'

12 Larbi Ben M'hidi, one of the founding members of the FLN (*Front de Libération Nationale*), declared of the series of terrorist attacks in Algiers in 1957: 'Give us your tanks and planes, and we will give you our cradles.' The reference is to the cradles in which the terrorists hid their bombs. He was tortured, then hanged, on 4 March 1957.

13 TN: The French words *ensauvagement* and *ensauvager* convey the idea of people returning to a wild or savage (i.e. pre-civilized) state. Politicians sometimes use this vocabulary in relation to ethnic minorities or working-class people when decrying a purported decline in moral standards or law and order.

14 A reference to the creative worlds of the rapper Booba and the rap duo PNL. See further below.

15 The title of a Zaidi El Batni song containing the line, 'Oh, France, what have you turned us into?' (*Ó France, qu'as-tu fait de nous?*).

2. Black Man Kills White Woman

1 Chester Himes, *The End of a Primitive*, London: Allison & Busby, 1990, p. 199.

2 Ibid., p. 201.

3 Ibid., p. 199.

4 Ibid., p. 198.

5 Ibid., p. 181.

6 Ibid., p. 201.

7 TN: This is a famous line from the classical tragedy *Phèdre* by Jean Racine.

8 Houria Bouteldja, *Whites, Jews, and Us: Toward a Politics of Revolutionary Love*, Los Angeles: Semiotext, 2017, p. 102.

9 Himes, *End of a Primitive*, p. 200.

10 Ibid., p. 201.

11 Ibid., p. 200.

12 Ibid., p. 199.

13 Ibid., p. 199.

14 Ibid., p. 200.

15 Toni Morrison, *Beloved*, New York: Vintage Classics, 2022, p. 113.

16 Iveton and Audin, both of French descent, were killed by the French state as a result of their anticolonial activism.

17 Himes, *End of a Primitive*, p. 201.

18 Ibid., p. 199.

19 Ibid., p. 201.

20 Ibid., p. 201.

3. The Impossible Community of Tears

1 Ralph Ellison, *Invisible Man*, London: Penguin Essentials, 2014.

2 Ibid., p. 4.

3 Ibid., p. 4.

4 Ibid., p. 5.

5 A term associated with Elijah Muhammad, the leader of the Nation of Islam.

6 Ellison, *Invisible Man*, p. 5.

7 TN: A reference to the slogan and hashtag 'Je suis Charlie' adopted in the wake of the terrorist attack on the offices of the satirical magazine *Charlie Hebdo*.

4. The Life and Death of Marcelin Deschamps

1 'De l'innocence blanche et de l'ensauvagement indigène: ne pas réveiller le monstre qui sommeille' (On white innocence and the regression into savagery of the native: don't wake up the slumbering monster), Parti des Indigènes de la République website, posted on 10 September 2019.

2 TN: A phrase popularized by the book *Les Territoires perdus*

de la République – antisémitisme, racisme et sexisme en milieu scolaire (Paris: Mille et Une Nuits, 2002), originally referring to the situation in French schools but now tending to denote areas of the country where law and order have purportedly broken down.

3 See the photo (cited below) of Zyed Benna (17) and Bouna Traoré (15), who were electrocuted at a power substation trying to avoid a police stop-and-search in the north-eastern Parisian suburb of Clichy-sous-Bois in 2005. Their deaths sparked the riots of 2005. See Angelique Chrisafis, 'French police to stand trial over death of two youths that sparked 2005 riots', *Guardian*, 20 September 2013.

4 Frédéric Mitterrand, *La Récréation*, Paris: Robert Laffont, 2013.

5 Mehdi Meklat, Facebook post, 20 February 2017.

6 Mehdi Meklat, *Autopsie*, Paris: Grasset, 2018.

7 'You can't have the beauty and depth of such literature and the hideousness of such thoughts residing in the same mind. We need to purge, clean out, scrape clean.' Christiane Taubira, Facebook post, 20 February 2017.

8 Meklat, *Autopsie*, p. 128.

9 Ibid., p.130.

10 Ibid., p. 38.

11 Ibid., pp. 38–9. TN: France Inter is a leading current affairs and cultural radio station for which Mehdi and Badrou worked.

12 Ibid., pp. 80–1.

13 Ibid., p.130. TN: The colours are those of the French flag.

14 In the wake of the murder of the schoolteacher Samuel Paty, the public intellectual Pascal Bruckner spoke on France Inter of his fear that some deranged individual would attack a mosque, because then 'we would lose the moral high ground'.

15 Meklat, *Autopsie*, p. 154.

16 Jean-Paul Sartre, Preface to Frantz Fanon, *The Wretched of the Earth*, translated by Richard Philcox, New York: Grove Press, 2004, p. xiviii.

17 Mouloud Achour to Meklat, quoted in *Autopsie*, p. 131.

18 Ibid., p. 155.

19 Ibid., p. 121.

5. Ounga Ounga

1 'La juge m'a dit "Pourquoi t'as fait ça?"/Ounga ounga ounga, ounga/ Caramel, moula, le nougat,/ voilà pourquoi, madre puta.' Booba, 'Nougat', *Trône*, 2017.

2 'Devant les profs, j'faisais des grimaces en tirant sur mon oinj, car on m'a dit en classe que l'Homme venait du singe.' Booba, 'Pitbull', *Ouest Side*, 2006.

3 Thomas Ravier, 'Booba ou le démon des images' (Booba or the Image Demon), *La Nouvelle Revue française*, October 2003, p. 40.

4 TN: An amalgam of metaphor and gore.

5 'Va t'faire niquer, toi et tes livres', Lunatic and Mala, 'Hommes de l'ombre', 2001.

6 'Énervé dans le 92 izi, car fouetté dans le Mississippi'. Booba, 'A3', *Autopsie vol. 3*, 2009. TN: The number 92 refers to the postcode of the Hauts-de-Seine department in the south-western suburbs of Paris where Booba grew up.

7 'Tout commence dans la cour de récréation. Malabar, Choco BN, "sale Noir!", ma génération'. Booba, 'Pitbull', *Ouest side*, 2006. TN: Malabar and Choco BN are brands of chewing gum and chocolate biscuit respectively.

8 Booba, 'Ma Définition', *Temps mort*, 2002.

9 Booba, 'Drapeau noir', *Trône*, 2017.

10 Booba, 'Ma Définition'.

11 Booba, 'N° 10', *Panthéon*, 2004.

12 This description comes from the missionary Eudofilo Alvarez, quoted by Mondher Kilani in *Du goût de l'autre, fragments d'un discours cannibale*, Paris: Le Seuil, 2018, p. 46.

13 Stella Magliani-Belkacem and Félix Boggio Éwanjé-Épée, 'Rester fidèle *au sang*: sur Sara Sadik' (Remaining loyal *to the blood*: on Sara Sadik), *Diacritik*, 23 September 2021: 'She wants to enlarge the images of her own people. Like in *Zetla Zone* (2019), where she creates an oasis in a desert. She invents superpowers borrowed from the Saiyans of *Dragon Ball Z* and the UFO of Jul, she turns Oasis and Capri-Sun soft drinks into wonderful elixirs. Sara Sadik works in augmented reality; she fashions worlds in which fantastical or futurist

motifs offer "extraordinary bodies" other ways of getting to know, recognizing, meeting and loving each other.'

14 Booba, 'Comme Une Etoile', *Lunatic*, 2010.

15 Booba, 'Ma Définition'.

16 Tandem, '93 Hardcore', *Tandématique vol. 1*, 2004.

17 TN: A term – 'alien bodies' – used by the Algerian philosopher Sidi Mohammed Barkat to denote the unequal legal status of 'natives' under French colonial rule.

18 *On partira drapeau hissé, canon vissé, en bon soldat Frérot, pleure pas, au fond des océans, on se retrouvera.* Booba, 'Kayna', 2021.

6. Fucked for Life

1 PNL, 'Zoulou tchaing', *Deux Frères*, 2019.

2 TN: *Que La Famille* (Family Members Only) is the title of PNL's first EP.

3 PNL, 'Obligés De Prendre', *QLF*, 2015.

4 A PNL line – *mille eu' sous la semelle* – from 'Jusqu'au Dernier Gramme'.

5 *Hess* is an Arabic word for hardship.

6 PNL, 'Différents', *QLF*, 2015.

7 PNL, 'Autre Monde', *Deux Frères*, 2019.

8 PNL, 'Zoulou tchaing', *Deux Frères*, 2019

9 TN: Always used in the plural, *lovés* is a slang word for money.

10 PNL, 'Gala gala', *Que La Famille*, 2015.

11 PNL, 'Le Monde ou rien', *Le Monde chico*, 2015.

12 PNL, 'Chang', *Deux Frères*, 2019.

13 PNL, 'Blanka', *Deux Frères*, 2019.

14 Sefyu, 'Suis-Je le gardien de mon frère?', *Suis-Je le gardien de mon frère?*, 2008.

15 PNL, 'À L'Amnoniaque', *Deux Frères*, 2019.

16 PNL, 'La Misère est si belle', *Deux Frères*, 2019.

17 PNL, 'Obligés De Prendre', *Que La Famille*, 2015.

18 PNL, 'Le Monde ou rien', *Le Monde chico*, 2015.

19 PNL, 'Dans La Légende', *Dans La Légende*, 2016.

20 PNL, 'Hasta la vista', *Deux Frères*, 2019.
21 PNL, 'La Misère est si belle', *Deux Frères*, 2019.
22 In the 'Au DD' video, the brothers appear at the top of the Eiffel Tower.
23 PNL, 'Au DD', *Deux Frères*, 2019.
24 PNL, 'La Misère est si belle', *Deux Frères*, 2019.
25 PNL, 'Sibérie', *Deux Frères*, 2019.

7. The Path of Blame

1 TN: A reference to the *tirailleurs sénégalais*, an indigenous infantry corps of the French army in colonial times.
2 TN: *Ghorba* is an Arabic word meaning an intense longing for one's homeland.
3 Magliani-Belkacem and Boggio Éwanjé-Épée, 'Rester fidèle *au sang*'.
4 TN: Eric Zemmour is a journalist and media pundit who stood in France's 2022 presidential election on a far-right platform.
5 Ninho, 'Tout ira mieux', *M.I.L.S*, 2016.

Index